Snowbirds Guarding the Gold

RV Life & House-Sitting Adventures

By

Al Allaway

© 2002 by Al Allaway. All rights reserved.

No part of this book may be reproduced, stored in a retrieval system, or transmitted by any means, electronic, mechanical, photocopying, recording, or otherwise, without written permission from the author.

ISBN: 1-4033-3505-2 (e-book)
ISBN: 1-4033-3506-0 (Paperback)

This book is printed on acid free paper.

Second Edition, 2003

April 2, 2002
Yakima, Washington

This book is about two major adventures. First, the humors and challenges of the RV life-style; **to be, or not to be:...a Snowbird?** (Chapters 1-4). And, second, it is about some very weird (and different) life-styles which we encountered as "house-sitters". Situations which brought unbelievable laughter, and copius tears. (Starting in Chapter 5). Our pets adapted better than we did to this new life, and they are the thread which holds the whole book together.

The stories which follow are "mostly" true. Every event happened pretty much as narrated. Only the afterthoughts about what "might have been" are fictional. Of course, names have been changed and some locations slightly modified because of what a lawyer might call "The need for a disclaimer".

Our "fantasy" flies off into the sunset...

DEDICATED to the hundreds of helpful and humorous friends we have met while **"On-the-road"**.

Snowbirds Guarding the Gold
RV Life & House-Sitting Adventures

Part I

"On the Road, Again"

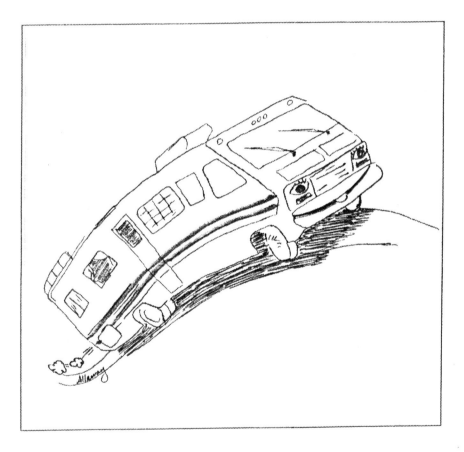

It was a "Happy" motorhome.

Al Allaway

Snowbirds Guarding the Gold
RV Life & House-Sitting Adventures

Chapter One: "The Bug Bites Hard"

(Ecclesiastes 3:1-7 "To everything there is a season, and a time to every purpose under heaven:...A time to keep silence, and a time to speak.")

Wind shook the new motorhome and horizontal sheets of rain were rattling like small buckshot. Through one blinding flash of lightning we could see huge pieces of the overhead fir trees sailing off into the stygian darkness. One severe gust of wind felt as though it was lifting our 31 foot motorhome up in order to follow the broken tree branches into oblivion. Then the thunder crashed!

"Meo r-r-r-ow!" screeched Fiesty, a pedigreed Siamese, as she buried her head under my armpit. Little did I realize then what a future mystery would be unfolding around this precious little cat.

Thunder crashed again, and Fiesty shivered deeper.

One of the wayward tree branches hit the roof of the rig with a thump, enough to make us all jump. Visions of 100 foot tall fir trees were crashing through the flimsy tin and fibreglass roof.

"It's okay, kitty," I said, stroking her quivering fur, "I won't let anything get you." Not quite sure if I could believe my claim.

Wife, Del who was also my lifelong best friend was saying a whispered prayer, "Mighty severe storm," I ventured, "I'll sure be glad to get out of here."

She continued her silent prayer, as two more fir boughs crashed onto the roof.

We were pretty much what you might consider to be "an ordinary family". When I retired from 26 ½ full years as a professional fire-fighter from Multnomah County and Portland, Oregon, we owned a modest ranch home in a nice wooded area of suburbia. All of the kids had grown up and moved on, hoping to find a new life pestering and interacting with some other unsuspecting adult humans.

We had kept ourselves actively busy with a wedding photography and consultation business, but the lure of the

"Open Road" and warm sunny skies started calling stronger within a year of leaving the Fire service.

Photography had always been a second love, but choice of subject matter was not always something a professional could control. Brides are especially fussy and always expect much more than they are willing to pay for. So after leaving several brides at the "altar" of Small-claims Court, we decided that a better choice of subject matter would be the more inanimate objects of pure Nature.

After all, I've never heard a wildflower complain, have you? And a glorious sunset never talks-back. When a brilliantly colored hummingbird buzzes by, one might think he was scolding, but if you really know birds, your brain can only hear and interpret the good sounds!

Well, that call of the wild kept getting louder and louder until one wet gloomy Fall day, Del woke me from a sunshiny dream.

"Hey, honey", she started, waiting briefly for the cobs to clear, "There's a neat motorhome for sale out in Beaverton that we should go look at."

Whoa!

And the call got louder. She was quick to remind that some years before, we had invested in a NACO-Thousand Trails camping membership, so with a motorhome, we could stay free at nice RV resorts.

Anything to get away from those fussy brides-to-be. Now, don't start ticking off the pros and the cons..."But, on the other hand..." "And, maybe if..." "However..." The bottom line is that we engaged a property control agent to rent our house, we sold or stored all the furniture and bought the motorhome, a slightly used 1985 Viscount by Mobile Traveler.

There is no way a writer can instill the *"Lure of the Snowbird"* life into the mind of a winter-ized "Norther", just like there is no way that one can understand the eternal "drizmal" rains of Portland and Seattle except through actual experience. You have to have been there to understand what a writer might be talking about. So it is, with doubts for the reader's full understanding of the concept, that I open up the following discussion.

Let's start with the phrase, "Balmy, warm breezes under swaying palm trees." Does that make a picture in your mind? How about Christmas Dinner with family on the patio? The only thing wrong with that picture is the lack of formal attire, because everyone is wearing shorts, sandals and tank tops. But, Christmas Day in Arizona or Florida is often in the balmy 70's.

It only cools off when your spouse announces, "The TV says to expect 12 more inches of snow tonight...(in Yakima, Washington)."

Then you can answer, "Ha, ha, ha, sure glad we're not up there."

And you think about poor Pete, your neighbor up North, who can't afford to repair his broken snow shovel.

"The last time I ever had to shovel any of that miserable white stuff was when we flew up north to visit your mother for Christmas and got caught in that freak six-day blizzard. I lost 10 pounds that week, remember?"

But, back to the motorhome. Pop the warm weather dream for a moment and get back to soggy Portland. It was mid-December, 1987 and our house was completely vacant; we were living in this 31 foot motorhome, parked in our driveway, waiting...waiting for the wind storm of the century to pass...waiting for more fir boughs to fall...And, waiting...

Waiting for a flu-like virus to die, so that some surgeon would feel safer poking electric needles in Del's back. Waiting...must have been over a week. At least we had an electric cord plugged in to the house and could keep the motorhome warm. And to keep from filling up the waste water tanks, we could return to the house for the necessary. But not in this violent wind...and the lightning flashed and the thunder crashed. And we waited, wishing we were back in our more secure vacant house.

Our ancient Siamese cat, Feisty was like all Pacific Northwest cats in the winter...cold-blooded. She used to snuggle under the foot of the comforter on our heated water bed, and dream her days away. Getting there was the funny part. She would bound down the hallway, round the corner and blindly leap onto the bed. It was comical; she didn't care whether the bed was made or not, or whether there was anybody in it or not, she just leapt and the devil could care how she landed. This became a habit for her because we had lived in that house for over eight years.

Mind-pictures of sugar-plum mice and warm water beds stay with a cat forever, so when the house was empty and the furniture was all gone, we could anticipate some fun, everytime we entered the house to use the bathroom. Feisty would be right behind us at the front door, then gallop down the hallway like a flash and do her leap thing. Her cry of dispair and disappointment was always worth a laugh, poor cat! She'd meow back at us saying, "What the heck did you do with my waterbed?"

I should have set up a camera with a remote in the bedroom, just to catch her flying through the air and landing on nothing. I guess the minds-eye picture of that invisible waterbed stayed with her until she died six years later, at age twenty-two years young.

We would sometimes stay in the house, killing time, for up to ½ hour, with no place to sit down. That was because it was the only way we could escape from the reverberation of the pounding relentless rain as it echoed through the motorhome, often so loud as to make normal converstion impossible. Even without the waterbed, it was a real challenge to get Feisty out of the house and back to real life.

For reasons unremembered, we had to ride out that severe storm in the motorhome, which like all traumatic events, finally came to an end. Unbelievably, none of the three large fir boughs caused any noticeable damage, except to our nerves.

Then the waiting ended, the virus died, and the surgeon did his job. Afterwards. he told Del, "Come back in two weeks, and we'll have a looksee at that incision".

Ha!

Because it was three days until Christmas and we'd had enough of the rain and wind and the waiting scene, is was easy to decide that the surgeon would never ever see that incision, so the following morning, the big adventure began. The cast of characters, in order of appearance, were Fiesty the Siamese cat, Daddy Al the author, Del the First mate, and Cindy, a sweet, but nervous Silky Terrier.

Our day for goodbyes to the neighbors is not one they'll soon forget.

We all lived on a steep dead-end street, which because of turning radius, provided no place to turn around our large motorhome, so, from the intersection at the bottom of the hill, it was easiest to just back the rig up to our curb.

Al Allaway

On the morning of departure, I had to make one last trip down to U-Haul because they had forgotten to provide an all important hitch pin which was needed to tow our little car.

When I returned for Del and the car, we had an opportunity to try out our newly acquired walkie-talkies, which had been purchased especially for use to assist in backing up in blind spots.

Down at the bottom, I honked to let Del know I was ready to back up the hill, and I saw her standing in the middle of the street, walkie-talkie in hand, ready to guide me up.

"A little to the left," she said, to no avail "Al! Straighten it out…Go left!," she said again, as I backed closer and closer to the waiting car.

"Stop, Now!" she screamed, loud enough for the whole neighborhood to hear, "You're gonna smash the car!"

Seems that one of us had forgot to turn our radio unit on. Do I have to say who? The car was spared, but everybody's nerves were not.

Oh, well!

Southbound at last!

Chapter Two: "Southbound to Sunshine"

(I Peter 4:9-10 "Use hospitality one to another without grudging. As every man hath received the gift, even so, minister the same one to another.")

Al Allaway

Feisty was terrified. The interior of any motor vehicle is usually anathema for cats. First, with visions of warm water beds dancing in her mind, she tried the queen size island bed in the motorhome. Under the comforter, she felt safe from all those fuzzy horrible images hurtling by…Hiding her head would stop the threat of fast moving trees and telephone poles. To her cat brain, they were always coming straight at her, in a blur. Threatening…Terrifying…Whizzing past too fast for a feline eye to focus on.

Every rear bed in a Class A motorhome is aft of the back axle, so vibrations and road bumps are greatly amplified. While we had been parked in front of the house, Feisty had thoroughly explored the coach and had eventually settled on the underside of the comforter as her future base of operations.

Thus it was on that cold drippy December morning of first departure, the poor cat, worn out from the previous night's terrifying wind storm, was sound asleep under the comforter, dreaming about her lost warm waterbed.

The first road bump was a gentle one, passing almost unnoticed. But the next one got everyone's attention and was followed by this most eerie cat scream that made the little hairs on the back of our necks stand up. Then came Fiesty, at a full gallop, bounding into Del's lap. The next instant, her head was buried under Del's armpit and her claws drawing blood from

Del's breast. I don't remember who was screaming the loudest, but my startled driving almost put the motorhome in the ditch.

That Darn Cat entered into the world of motorhome travel like no other, and would continue amazing us with her antics for the next six years.

Feisty's was not the only traumatic initiation to occur during this Christmas week of 1987. It had not stopped raining for over two weeks, and our hope of leaving the rotton weather behind, soon diminished. Just after crossing the California state line on US 101, the heavens opened up even more. Now, US 101 through the northern Redwoods was two and sometimes only three lanes (but never four). Add the gloom of deep woods and the glare of oncoming head lights through the pounding rain and the fog-like spray from other vehicles and you will have set the stage for the next trauma…

Wet pavement and steamed up windshields have a way of making highway lane markings invisible, which usually doesn't bother experienced drivers. But, you must know that this motorhome adventure had just started, and I had driven the heavy monster less than 500 practice miles. I'd almost swear that the motorhome felt like it was two lanes wide and a half a mile in length.

Oh, yes, let's not forget to add the extra traffic of Friday (and Christmas Eve) into this dismal formula. This was our longest day so far, and by the time we arrived at a NACO RV resort near Windsor, CA, I was shaking so badly that Del thought she would have to drive me to a hospital.

The title of this Chapter was "Southbound to Sunshine", but we were still looking for anything resembling the sun...

There was other warmth, however, as the good people of the RV resort learned that we were fresh newcomers. Park staff was shutdown for the Holiday, but four or five couples got a welcome party rounded up for us that very next day. Our first Christmas away from family was one we shall never forget. We were made to feel most welcome with Christmas hymns, and we happily joined in their hastily arranged prayer and praise celebration of this most holy day.

Hats off to Orval and Margerie Anderson (Home-based at The Dalles, OR).

A log, written at the time of these travels, contains much in the way of picky details which we will not bore you with. Most RVr's keep one like it, so they can settle future arguments like, "Where did we spend our 20th anniversary?"

But, we did finally find the sun and 50° "heat" a week later near Santa Barbara. Old Sol soon became a good friend.

Every RVer reading this already knows their own personal answers to the problems of on-the-road living. Problems like mail, phones, and banking. Much has been written on the various ingenious ways these problems have been solved, so we don't need to open any of those debatable bait boxes.

Once the sun came out, many photo opportunities opened up. Additions to an already huge nature slide collection were made in and around Southern California at places like Santa Barbara, Acton, Riverside, Hemet, San Diego., Yucca Valley, Idyllwild, Earp and Indio.

The only reason we even considered Yuma, AZ on our itinerary was because Del's mother and step-dad had fallen in love with the place and used it as their annual base for snowbird operations.

We had visited them there in November of 1978, on our honeymoon, almost 10 years earlier.

"What in blazes do they see in this God-forsaken sand-trap," I had asked Del.

"Hush," she said, "We'll just visit a few days and then head east towards New Mexico." Over east was the lure of real desert scenery, unusual and rare birds, tall cacti, wildflowers and rugged mountains.

"Okay," I agreed, "But only for three days!"

Ha!

Del's mom, Laura was in an exclusive little RV park which was full up, so we had to find accomodations somewhere else.

One of the free "perks" of our camping membership was the addition of three nights stay at other associated RV clubs called "Camp Coast to Coast".

And Yuma had one of those, a part of the Colorado River Adventures, named Yuma Lakes. Only trouble was that is was twenty miles out on the other side of town, away from mom.

It was a really nice park with pool, a fishing lake and lots going on. We enjoyed visiting mom and our three day stay and were prepared to leave, when the manager, George came knocking.

"How'd you like to stay on awhile?" he inquired.

"Can't do it," I said, "Your rules only allow three nights."

"Rules can bend," George replied, "I need a night security person, and the job is yours, if you want it."

How is it that such little things can have such an impact on the unknown future?

Del said, "Sure, sounds good."

"Okay," I agreed, "We can stay on for three more weeks, then we have to be in Gallup to welcome a brand new grand daughter."

So a deal was struck, three weeks free rent and all we had to do was direct late-comers to an RV space and lock up the pool enclosure at 10 pm. What could be sweeter?

It was during this time when we met our first skunks.

One evening, especially warm and muggy, we were late locking up due to a special party. Just before midnight, we encountered a little black and white "flower" out near the pool.

Part of the recreation area was fenced on three sides, and the skunk was pacing back and forth because it couldn't make up it's mind whether it wanted to play horse shoes or shuffleboard...So Del said, "Quick, Al, go back to the motor home and get your camera, and I'll sit right here and watch where it goes."

Well, when I came back, she was still sitting there, white as a sheet! I never did get the whole story, but it seems that another skunk, probably the mate, came around the corner, less than a foot away from where she was sitting, and rubbed up against her ankle, just like a puddy tat!

At least, this was the verbal excuse used in later slide shows to explain the lousy photo I had to use of a skunk.

We didn't know it yet, but our whole future had shifted into a different gear there at Yuma Lakes. And before those three weeks were up, George liked us so much, we had been hired for the next 6-month season, which would start October 1st, 1988.

After visiting my first grand daughter, Kathleen Marie Kuiawa, we spent much of the remainder of the Spring making repairs to our used motorhome, and did manage some nice scenery in Arizona, New Mexico, Utah, Montana and Idaho, returning to Portland in time for Summer!

Waukeena Falls picnic area, in the Columbia Gorge east of Portland is administered by the U. S. Forest Service and this year they got the bright idea to try out an RV live-in "Information Host".

We were hired for the job. Trouble was that there were no RV hookups of any kind for that first year the USFS chose to "experiment" with the idea.

It was an idyllic life, broken only on nice days by hundreds of tour buses with people from all over the globe.

The Forest Service had outfitted me with a Smokey Bear vest and campaign hat to enhance my trash picking-up device. The "reacher" was so fine tuned that I could pick up small bits of trash and cigarette butts with little effort. I got really proficient with the device, which often accounted for an hour or more of my time on every workday.

Trying to be friendly and helpful to hundreds of dumb tourists can wear down one's self esteem, and one day I blew it.

"What d'ya do with all those cigarette butts you're picking up?" asked one obnoxious tourist.

"Oh, we recycle them back to the tobacco companies," I replied with a straight face.

The poor guy must have believed me, because he headed for the nearest trash can, and dumped his remaining smokes.

On another busy day I was feeling somewhat authoritative when I observed a slob pitch his finished cigarette butt into the creek.

"Go get it", I demanded, as a crowd began to gather.

"But, I'll get my feet wet," the man complained.

"Tough", says I, "You should have known better than to litter in this stream."

To my surprise (and relief), he complied, like a puppy dog with his tail between his legs and stumbled and sloshed his way over slippery rocks to retrieve the wayward cigarette butt.

I wasn't aware of the large crowd that had gathered on the terrace overlooking this exchange, until the loud applause began.

Looking up, I was startled to see my audience; a whole busload of Japanese tourists, who had taken in the whole event with glee. They say that Japan has never had litter-bugs.

Enough, already! This was too embarrasing.

There was no salary with this job, and we had to drive out every week to dump our waste water tanks and to get a shower, but it was an experience. I made almost $200 that summer in recycled aluminum cans and cash found when cleaning restrooms. Ugh!

The next couple of years passed swiftly in a new Bounder motorhome while we phased our activities in the direction toward the entertainment and ministry fields.

Al Allaway

Feisty accepted the new motorhome with the grace that only a true people-lover could. And it was a whole three feet longer now, requiring an extra long leap in order to reach the bed.

Chapter Three: "This is God, Calling..."

(Psalm 77:1 "I cried unto God with my voice, even unto God with my voice, and he gave ear unto me.")

Yuma, Arizona on October 1st was still sweltering in the vicinity of 105°F. The summer monsoons had passed and humidity was becoming tolerable again. It was Nature's signal for the Snowbirds to **begin** their southbound migration.

Al Allaway

While many won't arrive for yet another month or two, park staff, including rest-room janitors, were expected to be in the park and fully prepared for "duty".

George, the manager had an unexpected surprise for us that day, as we were settling the motorhome down for a six-month stay.

For cleaning three separate shower-restroom buildings and one laundry room, we were to get a cash salary in addition to free rent.

Life was laid-back and lazy that first month, in fact one might call it a little boring. The park was only about 10% full and the restrooms stayed clean pretty much all by themselves. The activities staff had not yet come aboard, so for those few early birds, there wasn't much to do. We volunteered to organize a couple potluck dinners, and dipped into our video movie collection, and put on an old classic motion picture every night down at the clubhouse. We also helped organize a camper's worship service for Sunday mornings.

We had been assigned a site right next door to the park's Pastor, Clay Fultz and his wife, Janette, wonderful friends.

It was about then that we first got in trouble with the Activity Director, who arrived for duty about the end of October. Instead of a movie every night, Clay & Janette and some other folks who knew about my huge collection of nature photo slides, had talked me into doing a professional presentation every Friday night about the surrounding desert and it's varied wildflowers.

"You can maybe get away with a little Scripture hidden here and there," Clay had suggested, "But go easy because this is basically a non-Christian park, and we don't want to get us thrown out of here."

Most of the script was written right there to create our first production, **"Springtime on the Yuma** (Sonoran) **Desert"**. It was so well received, that we were packing the clubhouse with standing room only on the Friday when Activities first showed up for work.

"I had something else planned," she complained, "Are you trying to wreck my reputation before I can even begin my job?"

"Sorry, Bethe," I replied, "You weren't here and this seems to be what they all want…"

"Well, I'm the boss and we'll just see about that!"

I don't know what gets into some people, people who are always complaining that nobody will volunteer to help, but are never satisfied with volunteers who do try to answer their call.

Turns out, Bethe had to back down due to pressure from the residents. So, the dance schedule was set up for every other Friday, to alternate with that "Springtime Wildflower junk". I don't remember ever seeing her in attendance at a slide show, even after we added a sound track with music, bird calls and special effects.

But, the pool players and football fans still won out on Sunday mornings, restricting our church services to barely half an hour.

Now, there are over 100 RV resorts and trailer parks in Yuma, to accommodate the swelling winter-visitor population of more than 40,000 extra people. A dozen or so were huge complex resorts, boasting 800 or more RV sites each.

So, if **"Springtime on the Sonoran Desert"** was such a big hit in one park, why not try the others? Passing the "kitty" had already yielded an average of $40. per show. So we felt that it was time to branch out.

In all, eleven different programs were written, produced and photographed during the next few years. Themes about Nature's beauty, historical fact or fiction, and Christian Inspiration were developed., all with licensed music, sound effects and live narration.

As one might suspect, most of the RV resorts were somewhat dead set against any political or religious themes. We had to also develop some comedy routines to keep folks entertained until everyone was seated.

First used was someone else's material from a story about the hazards and problems RV'rs encounter at the dump station, which was a great comedy routine. We met many wonderful and talented entertainers when we were on the circuit. This particular show was created by some folks in Cloverdale, Oregon.

For the following two years, we set up an on-the-road itinerary with bookings in San Diego, Riverside, Hemet, Palm Springs, Indio, ElCentro, Yuma, Mesa, Apache Junction and Tucson. It was a busy time. Programs now numbered six and added titles like, **"The Cascades of Oregon & Washington", "Something About Yuma, Past & Present", "Wildflowers of the West", "Images of the Desert in Light & Shadow",** and **"And Let the Heavens Declare..."**. Bookings were so numerous that many days involved doing shows in two separate locations, with a few rare days of three.

At these 55+ senior parks, it was an accepted "standard" that nobody ever showed up on time for a program, so the pre-program stories and jokes became more and more necessary, while we waited for the stragglers. One of our favorites, written by a "Mr. Anonymous", was about the "BC" and went like this:

"Being a firm believer that humor is the spice of life, I'd like to pass on an amusing story first told by a Pastor's wife, entitled "The Travelers". This Pastor's wife had a friend who was a rather old fashioned lady, somewhat elegant and especially delicate in her speech. She and her husband were planning a week's vacation out in the unknown West, so she wrote to a campground resort to make reservations. She wanted to ask about the adequacy of their toilet facilities, but couldn't bring herself to write the word, "toilet". She finally came up with the phrase, "Bathroom

Al Allaway

Commode", but still thought that was too forward, so she merely referred to it as the "BC".

Well, the campground manager just couldn't figure out what the lady was talking about, and finally came to the conclusion that she was inquiring about the location of the nearest Baptist Church; the "BC", so he sat down and wrote the lady the following reply:

> *Dear Madam:*
>
> *I take the pleasue of informing you that our "BC" is located only nine miles west of our resort and is capable of seating 250 people at one time. I admit that is quite a distance away...especially if you are in the habit of going regularly, but you will no doubt be pleased to know that a great number of people take their lunches along and make a day of it. They usually arrive early and stay late. The last time my wife and I went was six weeks ago, and it was so crowded we had to stand up the whole time we were there.*
>
> *It might interest you to know that a supper is being planned to raise money to buy more seats.*
>
> *I would like to say that it pains me very much not to be able to go more regularly, but as we grow older it seems to become more of an effort, particularly in cold and wet weather.*
>
> *If you should come to our campground resort, perhaps I could go with you the first time you go, and sit with you, and introduce you to all the other folks,*

because, after all, ___(Name this park)___ is a very friendly campground resort!"

A little play-acting and the proper "timing" in reading the above letter, always got a good laugh, and helped loosen people up.

God's whispered call was now getting louder. The choosing of 88 verses of Scripture for **"And Let the Heavens Declare..."** was certainly done with some Divine intervention. Earlier, I had "heard" His call to do some Inspirational Praise and Worship programs, using slides of His beautiful Creation. But, as often happens with encounters with God, there was no further instruction on the how-to and where-from keys to the equation.

Another full year passed while I concentrated on reading the Bible through again from cover to cover. This time, I made 3x5 file cards of any Bible verse which might possibly apply; ending the year with over 500 index cards.

"Now, what, Lord?" I prayed.

No apparent or obvious answer! Was God asleep?

"Come on," I pleaded, "I can't do this by myself."

The cards had been loosely stacked in chronological order starting with Genesis and ending with Revelation. They made a tall tower on mom's old wobbly legged card table, and who should come bounding down the hall about that time? Fiesty, and the cards went flying in all directions.

"That Darn Cat never ran into a table leg before; what's wrong with her?"

And I then had to consider playing 552 card pick-up. And how to get them all back in order? But, before I strangled the cat, it dawned on me that maybe there was an easier way...

Considering that the general outline was to include seven major parts, this appeared to be as good a time as any to sort verses into seven random piles, such as: <u>Love</u>; <u>Creation</u>; <u>Glory</u>; <u>Nature</u>; <u>Praise</u>; <u>Strength</u>; and <u>Hope</u>.

"Okay, how does having seven piles of scripture cards instead of one get me any closer to an answer?" I asked myself, but really sending the thought waves up to my Father, who still appeared to be ignoring me.

"Put it away for awhile," suggested Del, "You're trying too hard; let it rest."

"But..."

The phone rang, it was my mother.

"How about coming over for some gin rummy?" she pleaded, "I'm lonesome, today."

Mom had been raised in a very strict Puritan Christian home where cards were an absolute "no-no". But like many people, she had rebelled and allowed the pendulum of her life to swing the exact opposite direction. In her retirement, Mom lived for her cards, for bingo, any games of chance, and dreams of breaking Las Vegas.

"Okay, Mom," I replied, "Just as soon as I solve this problem that's been buggin' me".

"What kind of problem?"

I explained about the scripture cards.

"That's simple," she continued, "Just shuffle each stack and use them however they fall."

Whoa!

Now, I've always had a good dose of Faith in God, so it didn't take long for Mom's idea to germinate into a worthwhile solution.

So I said, "Okay, Lord, how about this?" "We shuffle each category three times, and trust You to put the Scriptures in an acceptable order." I suggested a rule that I could by-pass any card that didn't seem to fit the pictures or the music, and put it back on the bottom of the deck. Otherwise, all cards had to be used in whatever order they ended up.

The amazing thing is that it worked! Pastors of churches were asking me years later how I ever had managed to create such an agreeable blend of verse. But, we know who did all the work, don't we?

God had sent an answer to my plea for help in the form of a tiny little Siamese cat named Fiesty. She had never been so

Al Allaway

clumsy as to run blindly into a table leg before or anytime afterwards, either.

And Mom could never admit that God might have used her as well.

God rest them both!

Snowbirds Guarding the Gold
RV Life & House-Sitting Adventures

Chapter Four: "Here Kitty, Kitty, Kitty...Time To Go"

(Proverb 18:4 "The words of a man's mouth are as deep waters, and the wellspring of wisdom as a flowing brook.")

Feisty learned to love the RV life-style so much, that when it was time to pull the "plug" she was usually rarin' to go! Usually...

Her first aggravating upset of our time-schedule occurred in rainy Seattle.

We were visiting Del's daughter, Valerie for Thanksgiving and had been parked in her driveway for a couple of days. Our time frame was a little tight, because Val was expecting her dad and his motorhome the next day. And for reasons I don't need to explain, Del did not want to be there when her ex-husband arrived.

Feisty had been raised in Portland, so Seattle's never ending rain was nothing new. She prowled the neighborhood, as usual, doing her cat thing.

We can only surmise what happened next...In the pouring rain, Fiesty dashed from backyard out-building to shed or whatever, and found an open door and a dry warm place. Such a place is always a signal to a cat that it is nap time. Fiesty obliged, and while she napped, some unsuspecting human came along and innocently closed a door, trapping the cat inside.

"It's 8:00 AM, and we better hit the road," I said to no one in particular, as we hugged family good-bye.

"Is Fiesty aboard?"

"Dunno, didn't you let her in?"

"Not me..."

"Here, kitty, kitty, kitty..."

That Darn Cat!

We spent an extra unplanned day, fighting with our inner selves, but knowing that we loved that little cat too much to drive off and leave her. And the irony of it all was that she used to be Del's ex-husband's cat anyway.

Well, after Feisty figured we were sufficiently worried, she showed up just before dinner time, so we couldn't leave until the following morning (Betch'a can't guess how very very early?).

It's a good thing that Val's dad was a day late! But, we got an early enough start that we missed him.

Feisty was a different sort of a cat; she was **afraid of mice!** We had learned about her phobia when we were still living in the ranch house deep in the woods of Gresham, before we sprouted our Snowbird wings. One day, Cindy, our Silky Terrier started "digging" and barking at the base of a recliner in the family room. Feisty, asleep in the chair ignored her, and we assumed that Cindy was just teasing the cat, or trying to get her to play. But Cindy wouldn't relent and started whining and seriously scratching the rug. She gave the impression that there was a doggie treat caught under the chair, so in order to shut her up, I shooed Feisty off the chair and turned it over to get the "treat". Turns out the "treat" was a hiding house mouse, which the dog promptly caught, while the cat took off in the opposite direction.

Much later we had traded in the old motorhome on a new 34' Bounder.

It had a large flat dashboard, and Feisty would sit up there in front of Del, watching the road, as if to say, "Where we going next, Mom?" This new motorhome (1989) also had the rear-axle island queen bed, and because of the on-the-road vibrations, was a little shop of horrors for Fiesty.

As soon as we'd stop for the night, she'd be off to explore the neighborhood. One night near the Strawberry river in east Utah, she got badly beaten up by a couple of raccoons, so we decided it was time to wean her to a cat leash...!

No way!

Step One: Buy a kitty halter. Step Two: Attach to cat! Step Three: Pick up cat who is playing "dead-dog". Step Four: Throw halter and leash into the trash.

Bad idea!

Every time we set her on her feet, trying out the halter, she'd simply fall over on her side and get all stiff. Try it again and she'd fall over on the opposite side. Our Silky Terrier, Cindy would race around this little scene, barking her encouragement.

"Gimme my leash," I thought she said, "And I'll show this stupid cat how to do it!"

Feisty had more brains than anyone was willing to admit, especially Cindy.

Too bad, too, because some RV parks had rules about cats. We learned early to wait until dark before letting her out.

When traveling with an independent cat, Lesson Number One is: Never, ever figure on keeping any time schedules.

After six months in the same space at Yuma Lakes, we were always anxious to be "On-the-Road" again. We even had Willie Nelson's popular song of that title cued and ready to play, the minute we exited the gate. That first day out was planned to run like a smoothly oiled clockwork. It was 8:00 AM.

Checklist completed, I said to Del, "Let's roll!"

"Wait a minute; where's Fiesty?"

"Oh, no!"

I think a stroke or heart attack would have been more welcome, than the sinking feeling which just then happened in the pit of my gut.

That Darn Cat!

We searched, we called, we prayed, and we wept. We had everybody else searching too. We loved her as a part of our family; we loved her too much to drive off and possibly abandon her. Four hours later someone told us they thought they had seen her that morning going into the RV storage enclosure.

"Track down George to get a key," we said in unison.

"Can't," came the reply, "He's gone into town."

We ate lunch and kept searching.

At 3:00 PM, George returned and was informed of our plight. He shrugged, then laughed with a devilish and knowing gleam in his eye, but then opened the gate. and I headed for the only motorhome parked in storage. A faint meow answered my call. Feisty had crawled up underneath the motorhome into a dark void above the wheel well.

I called and called, and she answered from her day-napping place. I swear she said, "I don't want to leave this place!"

So here's the stand-off. I had to crawl under (In the hot sand) and have a look-see. About three feet up inside, I could barely make out her tail, slowly swishing back and forth.

"Ahah", thought I, "If I can just reach up there and get that tail!"

"M-Re-e-eo-o-w!"

We were now a whole day behind our schedule, so scratch the itinerary.

Darn Cat! It's a litter box for you from now on!

Once we got moving, however, Fiesty's rebellion ended and she forgave me for pulling her tail.

Another time, she was the main-line clown attraction of a busy rest-stop area. We were somewhere in the low (and hot) desert near Tucson where we had pulled off the road for a short stretch. There were about twenty other motorhomes and trailers lined up single file at curbside. Fiesty had been plotting escape because she'd had enough and her little cat brain had assumed we were stopping for the night.

What she didn't figure in her calculations was that it was over 100° Farenheit outside. She carefully hid herself by the air-conditioning vent, unseen under a chair near the door, waiting her chance.

"We can't take more than twenty minutes here," I reminded Del as I headed outside for a short jog.

Swish—ish!

"What was that?"

"Fiesty just ran under the motorhome."

"Darn Cat!"

The puzzle was now to get a stubborn, independent cat to come out from the shade, into the hot sun so we could recapture her.

You gotta be joking!

By now we had attracted several other snowbirds who, without exchanging any words, understood our plight. So, we had her surrounded on all sides.

"Maybe she'll come out if you start the engine", suggested one nice lady.

"Good idea," says I, "We'll try it."

The idea was so good, that you can now picture an increasing number of big people moving rear-ward from motorhome to fifth-wheel to motorhome chasing one tiny cat, right on down the line, trying to escape the noise and exhaust of newly starting engines.

To everything there is a season, and all things come to an end...

When she reached the last motorhome, she had no where else to go, except off the asphalt and into the hostile desert.

She made it about 20 feet, then stopped dead. You've seen a cat lift dainty paws when in water or snow. Well, this time it was either the scalding sand or desert thorns, or both, but it didn't take very long for her to decide this had been a bad place to plan any escape, and she was gratefully back in our rig, nursing her sore feet next to the air conditioning vent.

I never did go jogging that day.

Like I said earlier, that Darn Cat adjusted too well to the RV life-style!

We were true "full-timers" for a few more years. The slide-show circuit lasted for two full years; winter in the Southwest, summer in the Pacific Northwest.

The beginning of the end came in the spring of 1990 when my mom, living in Portland, began to hint at a health problem.

Time that summer hung heavy and we felt in total darkness as we nursed mom and moved her from one level of health care down to the next.

"Please, Lord," I would pray, "Give us a light at the end of this tunnel."

We found ourselves making many cancellations; breaking contracts for future slide-show bookings, etc.

We had been hired by Araby Acres (One of the larger RV resorts in Yuma) for maintenance work starting October 1st. Bless them, they understood our dilemma and held the job open for a couple of extra months. But by mid November, the only fair thing we could do was to give it up.

By the end of the year, mom would be gone, a victim of tobacco company profits and lung cancer. Our little Silky terrier, Cindy and our faithful tow car also died the same week.

We made it to Yuma in mid-January, only three and a half months late, to find NO JOBS and NO VACANCIES.

Yuma didn't see very much of us that year, for in March we headed east to "See the U.S.A." and created two new programs while driving through eleven midwest states, ending up back in Yakima. They were **"The Monumental Southwest"** and **"Along the Lewis & Clark Trail"**.

Feisty the cat really had settled down, enjoying the tour of the Nation, and when we bought our own lot in Yuma, she thought she was in Paradise.

The motorhome was still our only abode and had held up well. We put it on the market in 1994, but didn't sell it until 1997.

Our first lot in Yuma was traded in for a larger lot and a permanent "park model" in March of 1994, Feisty now had a new home to explore.

Al Allaway

The scariest experience we ever had on the road was in Eugene, OR in the middle of downtown Friday rush hour traffic.

There are very few service stations laid out with sufficient room for a long RV, especially one with a tow-vehicle attached. In some small towns, we were forced to drive on and trust to luck, or disconnect the tow car before getting gas.

We were on our last trip south, before selling the motorhome, and stopped for gas in Eugene.

It was one of those misaligned stations with a huge dip in the rain-gutter, where the driveway refused to meet the level of the city street. Traffic was heavy, so we had to pull out faster than normal in order to merge with rush-hour traffic.

When the tow bar passed over the gutter, the motorhome went one way, while the tow car bounced the other direction. The shock released the emergency catch causing the tow bar to separate from the ball-hitch. Only the safety chain was then connected. We then had to merge through four lanes of traffic in order to find a safe place to stop, and we learned how cranky those Eugene, Oregon drivers can be.

Fortunately, our damage was light, even after the car banged into the motorhome six or seven times. Del, however, was a little stressed after directing traffic around us while I manhandled the ball hitch and yoke back together again.

There were lots of other times when the damage was not so light, like the time we forgot to take down the TV antenna and took out a power line, or the time the electric steps failed to retract and did a number on the fire hydrant.

If you ever get bored sitting in a large RV park, just tune your CB radio to channel 14 after lunch when new arrivals are starting to back into their assigned spaces. It's a blast, especially listening to the fifth-wheel people. Ma gets out to inspect the site, while Pa gets lined up and ready to back in. Then you hear Ma on the radio, "A little to the left, honey."

"More to the left honey…No, No, go the other left!"

Pa, "My left or your left?"

Ma, "Just straighten it out!"

Crash!

"What was that?"

"You just hit a tree, dummy"

They know that everyone is listening, so when you meet that evening in the clubhouse, eye contact never happens!

Al Allaway

Snowbirds Guarding the Gold
RV Life & House-Sitting Adventures

Part II, "The House-sitting Lure"

Bootsue, the Shih-tzu

Al Allaway

Chapter Five: "Rules For House and Pet-Sitting"

(Matthew 5:44-45 "But I say unto you, Love your enemies, bless them that curse you, do good to them that hate you, and pray for them which despitefully use you, and persecute you; That ye may be the children of your Father which is in heaven: for he maketh his sun to rise on the evil and on the good, and sendeth rain on the just and on the unjust.")

Living full-time in a motorhome can offer a real challenge to that moth-ridden object we know as a pocketbook. The RV life-style dream never included the cost of paying rent every night, every place.

True, the enterprising traveler can find an occasional freebie at Wal-Mart, the Elks Lodge or a relative's driveway, but most of the time everybody else has their hand out. It's a sign of our times that one now pays more for an RV spot than we used to pay for a nice motel, pool, continental breakfast and all the other amenities. And half the time the RV spot isn't even full hookup!

Over the course of our adventures, we parked in many weird places and for varied reasons. "Watchman security" was the primary string attached to any "free" parking we ever encountered.

The year after our Campground "Hosting" at Waukeena Falls (see Chapter 2), we got a summer long job in Portland at the Mitchell Bros. truck terminal. In exchange for free parking and electric hookup we were "Quasi-security guards" inside a gated yard. Long-haul truckers arrived at all hours of the night, and would drive out in their private vehicles and forget to close the gate. There was one we remember who had no one waiting at home, and after three or four days on the road, would pull his rig into the yard at 3 am or so, looking for any human being he could find who would listen to his woes.

"Poor man is really lonesome," Del would say, "Be a good Christian and listen to his complaints…But he really scares me, too."

And guess who he "dumped on"? Sometime in mid July, he got put in jail for something, and we finally started getting some decent nights sleep.

Then, there was a couple of churches in the Morton, WA area who had serious troubles with night time vandals and were always willing to park us in their back lot whenever we were in the area. It made us feel really wanted when churches started to "fight" over us.

Feisty, the Siamese lasted until she was twenty-two years old. I don't know what that figures out to in cat years, but by dog standards, she lived a very full 140 years. She provided much companionship and many laughs. We certainly miss the dear, brave little cat.

In the spring of 1997, we still had not sold the motorhome and decided to try something new. The Yakima Herald-Republic had an advertising classification called Housesitting where we had seen several short ads. So we gave it a try:

Del had just had tendon surgery on both ankles and was in surgical boots and walking with crutches.

> **Retired Christian Couple** will sit your house or pets. Summer only 577-9954

"We have to go for an interview," I told her one morning. "There's a couple up in the west hills who are touring the east coast for a month and a half and might be able to use us."

"I sure hope they don't have any stairs," Del replied.

"It's a Colonel and Mrs. Lewis," I said, "And I think she said it was a three-story with daylight basement."

We had already mailed them our photo and a brief resume, which included this statement:

*"**About the House-sitting:** We move in with several bags of personal effects and live in your house, use your linens and dishes (But not your food). We keep things cleaned up, plants watered, lawn mowed, and are watchful of your security. We try to make friends with your pets (if any) and be sure they get proper care. From a list you furnish, we will call for and coordinate necessary emergency repairs. We take messages and forward mail, if desired. There is no charge, of course and all utility bills continue to be your responsibility. We would like access to your newspaper, telephone and computer, but not required. We are bondable and require a lot of information from you, including a meeting of at least one hour, several days before your departure. There is a list attached of things we need to know."*

The interview was successful and lasted over two hours. Lewis turned out to be a recently retired Colonel of the Air Force who had served his last hitch in *"Desert Storm"*. They were planning to drive back east, and spend much time with relatives and do some sight seeing, but weren't scheduled to leave for another month, yet.

Our first experience with this sort of an interview taught one important lesson, and that is that we need to know as much about strangers as they want to know about us.

Snowbirds Guarding the Gold
RV Life & House-Sitting Adventures

I can't truthfully say that this was to be our first house-sitting job, because while we waited for the Lewis's departure, we were in familiar territory, house-sitting for cousins Johnnie & Betty and their dogs, Humphrey Bogart, a medium sized Poodle and Squirt, a "mutt" that had never been housebroken. Bogey was half deaf and going blind. We parked our motorhome in their side driveway and ran an extension cord through the basement window, so we were not house-sitting technically but rather guarding the house and feeding the dogs. And for ten days fearfully anticipated the coming resposibilities of a real-job.

We had one more meeting with Col. & Mrs. Lewis, who by now were becoming friends, helping to ease our fears.

Greetings such as, "Let me show you how to use our computer." and "Do you like games like Mahjongg and Free-cell?" or "Here's a special password, so you can get on the Internet." Now, I ask you, how can anybody be fearful of strangers who are so giving and so friendly?

Peace be with you!

When you live in someone else's house, you can grow in the knowledge of the good points of the way other people live. Their ways can become your ways. Many good discoveries were made this way.

Everyday was an adventure in the discovery of something new, something interesting, and something not understood.

The Lewis's had no pets; live ones, that is. But the Colonel did have one peculiar fetish; he collected Teddy Bears! Not just a few, but thousands!

In the downstairs family room there were many war momentos hidden amongst the bears. Bears covered three walls, floor to ceiling, jammed into bookshelves, sometimes three deep.

On the wall nearby were a couple of photos of the command vehicle of the Colonel's armored unit, somewhere in the desert near the Iraq-Kuwait border. An excellent cartoon caricature near the photos showed a driver, the Colonel, a Staff officer, a Communications Sergeant, and TWENTY some-odd Teddys! In the background of the picture there's a column of tanks following their Commander. I never did figure out how an Air Force Colonel ended up in the field, commanding a tank battalion, or what kind of a nick-name his troops must have had for him. But, we won that war!

This wonderful adventure lasted for 45 days and we were not looking forward to their return.

There was an outdoor hot tub which we had to keep in chemical balance and clean, but only used twice.

There were raspberries ripening along the back by the canal.

Our new dog, a little Shih-tzu, named Boot-sue loved the freedom of her new back yard, except when I had to mow.

Del learned a new phrase, "Honey, you've been sitting at that computer for hours, won't you please come to bed?"

"Did you dust the teddy bears?"

"No, did you put the house-sitting ad back in the paper?"

Snore-re-re-re!

Our next job was miles away in an opposite end of the valley. We had stored the unsold motorhome in a consignment lot because there was no room for it at the Lewis's.

These new folks, named Tudor were motoring to Tennessee and their need for us dove-tailed perfectly with the return home of Col. Lewis. Besides which they had lots of room for our motohome.

The interview went very smoothly where I learned that they were Canadians. There was a good joke about the origin of the name Canada that I used to share with my slide show audiences, so I thought they would enjoy it too...

It went like this: *"..'Ave you heard 'ow they named Canada? It was a bright sunny day when all the natives gathered in a big meadow to decide what they should name this new country...After some discussion it was decided that they would put all the letters of the English alphabet into a big 'at, and draw them out one at a time, and name the land however the letters were drawn out of the hat.*

A hush fell over the crowd as the big moment arrived.

"C," called the announcer, "Is the first letter drawn...ay?"

"N, is next," he said, ".. Ay?"

"Third letter is D,….ay?"

And that's 'ow they named Canada; C…ay, N…ay, D…ay."

Some Canadians have a good sense of humor, others do not. But, we got the job anyway.

Eugene and Dolores Tudor had a little dog named Sassy, who made instant friendships with Bootsue. Our only problem was the sleeping arrangement; both dogs were used to sleeping on the bed with the "masters". But, we couldn't permit that because they pushed and shoved all night long and the Tudor's only had a standard double bed, certainly not big enough for four bodies!

"Poor Sassy's going to have to sleep in the guest room," I told Del the 2nd night, "I hope she'll be okay."

"No," she answered, "That wouldn't be fair. After all, this is Sassy's home."

After giving it a little thought, with the Wisdom of Soloman, I suggested, "Let's try this and put them *both* in the guest room." It was, I supposed, a brilliant suggestion.

Sassy thought she had reverted back to a puppy, because she whined all evening, looking for the comfort of the 'hot-water bottle". Bootsue responded with a shrill bark every few minutes. We couldn't decide if the bark was her way of telling us that it wouldn't work, or for Sassy to shut up.

About midnight all four of us on one bed, settled-in just fine.

The two previous house-jobs had physically helped to prepare me for the ardours of cutting grass. The Tudor property was over 3 acres in size, with one acre in alfalfa and vegetable garden, and the other two acres in lawn. And he wanted it mowed twice a week! Praise the Lord for power mowers!

There was a large shed where he kept the mower, and also a full sized tractor. Although the temptation to use it was strong, my activities were confined to the small power mower. That is, when the other occupants of the shed allowed me access.

The family of yellow jackets were the first to object. But powerful wasp sprays and time were soon on my side.

The other residents were given full run of the shed and left as undisturbed as possible. It was a family of striped skunks, *Mephitis mephitis*. After the first encounter, we gave each other wide berth. Their presence was repeatedly made know to us almost every night, especially when the wind was in their favor. It was an uneasy truce.

Eugene Tudor had forgotten to tell me about the neighborhood "Skunk lady", who made a great profit in this part of town. She'd come out and set traps, capture the skunks, de-scent them, then sell them for pets.

Al Allaway

When I was a kid in high school, the local museum had rental animals including several "pet" skunks, they would loan out to neighborhood kids to teach them care and compassion for animals. Once de-scented, they do make pretty nice pets.

Bootsue had her first experience learning to use a doggie door. She was a little slow at first, thinking that somebody else caused the door to open. It took several days for her to learn that it was her own weight that did the job.

Sassy would show her how, then bark encouragement. Once she finally got the hang of it, they'd play chase, in and out, out and in. Due to the presence of the skunks, we had to lock the door at night.

One of Eugene's hobbies was vehicle rebuilding, and part of our duties were to keep a detector eye out on a garage, which was several hundred yards from the house. In it he had restored an old Ford fire engine and several fine touring cars. He and Dolores, his wife entered and putt-putted in many local parades and the annual "Vintiques" competition. The building was disguised as an old Texaco service station, with gravity gas pump and all.

Along with the photography of birds and flowers, we've always been interested in small animals and insects, too.

One day, Del came screaming into the house.

"Get your camera, quick," she gasped, "I've found this huge bug...Hurry!"

It was a green-brown Praying mantis, a magnificent specimen almost seven inches long.

"Let's photograph it against something to show it's huge size," I said.

"Do they bite?" she asked.

"Don't think so," says I, "Pick it up and see."

There are times in our lives, when we know that we're about to do something stupid, and this was one of those times.

Del let the mantis crawl onto her finger so I could get a closeup picture…which never happened!

She let out a screech you could hear a mile away. The mantis was flung into the next county, and we both learned a valuable lesson.

Tudors had planted a vegetable garden of giants. I've never seen such huge sunflowers, squash, pumpkins, melons and tomatos, as they grew. And most of them fell dying on the ground, unwanted. We harvested as much as we could and shared much with our church. Summer was drawing to a cool close when they returned, and it wasn't much after that we headed south for another winter in Arizona.

Some of those huge sunflower seed heads went with us for birdseed, but Mother Nature played a mean trick on us. The Arizona songbirds had never seen sunflower seeds growing in such big heads, and were afraid to come near them. Most of

Al Allaway

the seeds rotted away, except those we hand picked, which the birds then greedily gobbled up.

Snowbirds Guarding the Gold
RV Life & House-Sitting Adventures

Chapter Six: "House-Sitters Are Nuts"

(Psalm 100:4 "Enter into his gates with thanksgiving, and into his courts with praise: be thankful unto him, and bless his name.")

Now it was Springtime of 1998, and we were imagining that we were beginning to learn something about the art of housesitting.

Ha!

The house-sitting ad was no longer running, as we were getting all our contacts now through referrals. Apparently Yakima has had a professional housesitting company for years, who charged a fee to care for pets and property. So, people like us, willing to take on such responsibilities for free were not very common, so our popularity increased overnight.

Al Allaway

"Do you realize that we might be making some enemies?" I asked Del one April day, as we motored west- bound out of Virginia.

"How so?" she replied.

"We've already got seven housesitting jobs lined up for this summer, and we're not even there, yet," I said, "And I worry that we might be putting someone else out of work…"

We were on the last leg of a grueling cross country trip where we had thought the shortest route from Arizona to Washington state was via Virginia. To add to the driver's stress, we were towing one compact car full of slide show equipment by a mini van which was not made for towing. This had been the year that our slide ministry had been requested in Virginia, Iowa and Idaho.

"If we had a full-time address, some of those regular professional housesitters could take out some revenge on our property," I continued. "Maybe we should keep an eye on our back trail…"

On May 27th, we checked in with the next "job". Not really a job at all, but a convenience to us because of the free lodging.

I've mulled over and over trying to find an appropriate fictional name, like we've used for all the previous home owners, but because these next folks became such good friends, and nothing unusual or different ever happened, I've decided, with permission, to use their real names; Bud and

Marilyn Penoyar. I first thought that even their address had a hidden message for us. They lived on Trails End Lane, NE of Yakima toward Naches. This home was on a high cliff overlooking the Naches River valley, just before the river poured through a gap into the Yakima Valley. The view was outstanding, and we would sit for hours on their deck admiring all the natural scenery that our great God provided; a gift given out of His love.

We sat for the Penoyars on four different occasions in 1998 and twice more the next year. In fact, we were told that we had a home away from home at any time, even when they were in residence.

Bud and Marilyn were "later life newlyweds" having a lot in common with Del and I (Who still consider ourselves newlyweds). They took lots of trips, usually in a fifth-wheel trailer. Once they even flew the Concorde to Russia for a five week tour. On shorter local trips, they would normally take their Yorkshire Terrier along. Her name was Princess Helene.

Just after we started sitting for them, they obtained a new Yorkie pup, which they named; Charlie. Now Charlie was more properly called Prince Charles, but was a little slow in the house breaking department, so they always left him home with us. Bootsue and Charlie became great friends and would romp in their orchard for hours.

Al Allaway

Yes, orchard; about 100 delicious apple trees and one yummy apricot. We were never around at apple harvest time, but did manage to eat all the apricots one year. Mmm! Better than prunes for what ails you!

Under the trees, Bud had planted lawn, which was regularly mowed, so it was a great place for the dogs to romp. But every once in a while, just when the play got interesting, Charlie would take off running like only a Yorkie can do. He was after the marmots and the ground squirrels, who loved to tease him just before they popped into their holes. Bootsue would get disgusted with him and bark, "What's the big deal?" Sorry Charlie!

We just loved it at the Penoyar's, as there was always something new to photograph. We had some spectacular time-exposed lightning shows, triple rainbows or moonlight reflecting off the river in the valley below. Fantastic shots!

When the marmots weren't putting on a show, there was a flock of night hawks which would. I had my photo tripod set up permanently on their large deck, ready for instant mounting of a camera to photograph the next surprise.

A couple of times, range fires burned in the area, and we pre-fire planned and were prepared for anything with garden hoses on standby and sprinklers at the ready.

We were devastated when they listed the house for sale, and we had to endure weekend "Open-house" with the Realtor. When sold, they moved to Florida.

In between stays at the Penoyar's we were "captured" by our first "Red Indians". Now, we know what is "politically correct" when speaking about minority races; and Del and I were both raised on or near a reservation; thus grew up with Native American children, so what we say following, is to be taken with a grain of light and sweet humor.

The job was for the family of Stan and Shirley Whitefox, full-blooded members of the Yakama Nation. They were sweet and sincere Christian people with six adopted Native children, living in a better-than-average older ranch style house (With a full basement). Keep in mind that the basement is an important part of the story.

The only member of this family who disliked the "white-eyes" was a dog named Bandit, who made it known immediately that if we were to be tolerated, it would be on his terms. Bandit and their numerous cats were never allowed inside the house, so we were able to keep his shaky truce.

Whitefox was allowed tribal privleges which would be illegal for us; he loaded a large U-Haul van with sky rockets and other large fireworks and headed down to the Celilo Reservation on the Columbia River to sell fireworks to the "crazy white-eyes" over the Independence Day weekend.

He claimed that there had been break-ins in the remote rural area around their home, and they needed security for the six days they would be away selling fireworks.

We would be guarding a fishing boat, the house and a garage full of junk, including four freezers stuffed full of salmon. The dog and two litters of kittens used the garage for their home.

Shirley explained the kitchen and the laundry to Del and added a warning.

"Keep out of the basement", she said. "It's a mess down there where our three teen age boys live."

Not much can be said about the luxury of the house. The kitchen was something out of the 1920's; barely wired with electricity. Many lights and switches didn't work. It was in stark contrast to the clean and modern facilities of prior tales.

The first night, we were just drifting off to sleep, when Del jabed me in the ribs.

"What was that?'" she cried, "I heard a noise!"

Listening, I heard nothing.

"Go to sleep", I soothed, "It's just new noises in a strange house".

"Tum, tum, tum…"

"There it is again," she shrieked, "Drums! Ghosts in the basement!"

"Argh…"

Thinking perhaps Bandit was happily beating his wagging tail against an old washtub or some such, I again refused to believe any thing out of the ordinary.

"Go to sleep, honey...It's almost 1:00 am."

Welcome silence.

2:00 am: "TUM, TUM, TUM, TUM" And two people sat straight up in bed, now wide awake.

"Gad! Those really are pow wow drums!!"

"Stay here while I investigate the basement."

Now, how do you tell the next part without laughing? I had earlier checked out the basement to satisfy my curiosity after Shirley's warning to Del. I knew that I must have shoes because of broken glass and cracked floor tiles. I had already overcome the smell of stale unwashed clothes and whatever else teen age boys hide from their mom, so after I dressed, I ventured downstairs.

Meanwhile, the drums and Indian chanting grew louder and louder.

I still laugh when I recall that night, and what I found: A portable stereo tape player with alarm-clock function. The tape was a fine version of **"The Mandaree Singers"** at a Walla Walla Pow-wow from the year before. I've just never figured out whether the boys set it up on purpose, or if it was just an "accident".

What fun it was to house-sit for strangers!

The Whitefox family returned a day earlier than scheduled, or perhaps I should say, night. It was 10 pm and we were in bed…Had to get up and get dressed and go find a motel.

"How come you're home so early?" I asked, somewhat grumpy and half asleep.

"Fireworks were in such demand that we sold out," was the reply, "You can stay the night on the sofa, if you need to…"

Thanks, but no thanks!

Stan continued, "Leave your stuff here if you like because we'll all be going salmon fishing in two days, and we'll need you again."

"What d'ya think?" I asked Del as we and Bootsue went looking for a motel, 25 miles away in town.

"I can't think, now," she replied, "Let's just find a motel that permits pets, and get some zzz's."

Two days later, we phoned Stan & Shirley for instructions.

"It'll be yet another day," we were told, "Come by around noon, tomorrow."

"What's the matter?" I thought to myself, "Aren't the darned fish biting yet?" Be patient, Al!

At noon the next day, we arrived, hoping they would be gone. No such luck! We sat around, feeling useless and in the way for three more hours.

"Good luck," I hollered as they drove off in their motorhome with boat in tow, "Catch a lot!"

Little did I realize what I was saying. You know that Native Americans don't have to have game licenses, and aren't restricted by fishing seasons and number limits. That's the reason there were four freezers full of prize salmon. What in the world did they need any more for?

Next day we had a horrendous thunder storm, and lost power for a couple hours. Two hot days later, I started smelling rotting fish, and upon checking the garage, determined that the thunder storm had caused a power surge and blew the circuits to the garage. By the time I got a power cord from the house hooked up to the freezers, the salmon was half thawed.

After the electrician restored the power to the top of the garage's utility pole, I poked around out there a little bit more and found another horror.

Three of the little kittens had got themselves tangled up in some old fishing nets. I managed to get one cut loose, but found the other two had been strangled for several hours, and were quite dead. An evil thought occurred to me then; would Stan even care about the kittens? Would he be angry with me for cutting up a good fishing net? And, would he even care about all the wasted salmon? I supposed not, and Mother Earth would cry another tear...

Lyric tales of Native American folklore contain many lessons, some of which were brought to mind with this house-sitting assignment.

Al Allaway

I was made to seriously consider the conflicts that have grown up in man's eternal struggle and relationship with "Mother Earth". The ecological battles can only worsen as the populations increase. And, it is not a problem to be considered only by Native Americans.

Just maybe the Whitefox family, like many others, took more from "Mother Earth" than they gave back. Perhaps Stan too, could take the cue, and learn something from a modern Indian lyric called Stumbling Bear!

We were indeed, glad to be finished with this Indian home and to return to civilization. They did, however, surprise us with a handsome monetary bonus.

The next (and last) job for 1998 was in mid September, just before Father-time's midnight stroke turned us back into Snowbirds.

We failed the first interview because these folks had three dogs, a young Cocker Spaniel, a middle aged German Shepherd, and a very old Golden Retriever. They felt that their dogs would never tolerate another dog (Our shih-tzu Bootsue) in the house. While their pets slept in an outdoor kennel, it was feared they would be jealous and attack our little dog.

After a month, they reconsidered and called us back for another interview. They'd had difficulty finding someone else to sit the house, so it was agreed that we'd lock Bootsue in the bedroom while we fed the "big three" in the kitchen.

That settled, Ray and Ruth Herlew took off on a 14 day trip, and we snuggled down in a very comfortable house, which included a weekly housekeeper. The dog feeding arrangement worked well for the big three, but Bootsue was not a happy camper, and the first day, she managed to push the bedroom door open and join the feeding frenzy.

We thought we had lost our dog, as we watched in horror as the drama unfolded.

But Bootsue simply growled at those big dogs, sniffed their food, refused it, and arrogantly ignored them. From that hour on, she was the alpha, the boss dog, and they towed the line. When we told the Herlew's, they couldn't believe it. We still lured the big three back into their kennels at night. This trick was accomplished with the help of five pounds of frozen hot dogs.

Chapter Seven: "All Creatures Great & Small"

(Genesis 1:25 "And God made the beast of the earth after his kind, and cattle after their kind, and every thing that creepeth upon the earth after his kind: and God saw that it was good.")

In the Yakama Indian Nation there are many different types of residents. There are the Native Americans who remain poor, usually as a result of low alcohol tolerance. These were mostly remembered from the early 50s wrapped in colorful blankets, sitting on the boardwalks of Wapato and Toppenish.

The next class were the middle income Natives who were usually hard working, non drinking people, like the Whitefox's of the previous chapter.

Then there were the well-to-do families; community leaders, like the next Indian family who hired us. They were CeeCee and Cindee Allen, names certainly not very Tribal.

CeeCee had been a moto-cross racer and had a huge shop where he built his own deisel motorhomes. This was his "hobby" to keep busy after his retirement. Their acreage was on a sage covered hilltop, surrounded by vineyards and mint farms. Like Whitefox, they were 25 to 30 miles from any town.

We were to house sit for 45 days, while they tested his latest motorhome by driving to Alaska and back.

This was our first experience with an electronic security system, and it was a constant source of worry. Allen's had a whole walk-in office inside what appeared to be a bank vault, with the house built around it. CeeCee said he had much Native American history and valuable art work stored there. The house was equipped with motion detectors, which were aimed too high for Bootsue to activate, or so we were told. We were given a cell phone to take with us anytime we were away from the property.

"The automatic dialer in the alarm system calls the cell phone, first", Cindee expained, "Then our son, then the neighbor, and if none of those answer, dials the number of the Tribal Police".

She continued, "The house is wired in such a way, that you can listen to any sounds or voices from inside the house when the phone goes off."

"Keep it charged, and always remember to take it with you when you leave," reminded CeeCee.

"You're sure Bootsue won't set it off?" I asked.

"Positive," answered CeeCee.

We bid good bye on a warm sunny Monday in June to CeeCee and Cindee, as they drove off in their $300,000 diesel motorhome headed for the wilds of Alaska. We were really looking forward to guarding their mansion and pretending to live like the "Rich & Famous" for the next month and a half.

"Wonder what our first surprise will be?" asked Del, as the motorhome dust settled on the quarter mile long driveway.

"Anything but drums," I said jokingly.

This home was a nature lover's paradise. We could sit in the living room at dusk and watch coyotes stalking pheasants and jack rabbits. Like an oasis in the desert, every bird imaginable was attracted to the green and moist gardens around the house. The weather was perfect, and we could leave windows open; open to allow sounds to alert us to the presence of some new bird or animal.

Thus it was that we awoke from a deep sleep and came straight out of bed at exactly 2:00 am, startled by a loud rapid drumming sound.

"What the 'eck was that?" we said in unison.

"Sounded like a jack-hammer," says I.

"Well, go take a look," says she.

After prowling around a bit, I located the source, then snickered to myself, wondering how long I could keep Del in suspense.

"Well?" she demanded, as I re-entered the bedroom.

"Did you keep the bed warm, honey?" I said, just before she hit me with the pillow.

"Al!"

"Okay," I surrendered, "Remember that clock on the sun-porch with all the bird calls?" I continued to explain that a different bird sound "chimes" every hour, and 2:00 o'clock was the *Woodpecker...!* We'd been so interested in the real sounds coming from outside on this first day, that we totally ignored the false ones coming from inside the house.

You better believe, that the "chime" was turned off the next night.

Lazy hours were spent lovingly tending Cindee's prize roses and other beautiful flowers. And their patch of lawn was so small, it could be mowed in less than twenty minutes a week, quite a contrast to other homes we had watched.

The Allen's had two large dogs, CeeDee and Missy. CeeDee was half coyote, barely tame. Both dogs were outside critters, free to roam during daylight, but locked into the six bay garage at night. They seemed willing enough to stay locked up after dinner. Both bore scars from fights with the real coyotes. CeeDee was named C. D. for "Cee's dog". CeeCee had adopted him after he strayed into the yard, probably rejected by his wild brothers.

Al Allaway

As I mentioned, windows were often left open, until the day got too hot. A pair of kingbirds built a nest right outside our bedroom window. We really weren't aware of it until after the baby birds hatched, then the squawks and squeaks forced an immediate window closure. As these babies later fledged, we got some excellent and useable photos for the slide shows.

After the first week, it was time to head into town for groceries. The nearest Fred Meyer supermarket was over 40 miles away in Yakima, so it was to be an excursion.

"Don't forget the cell phone," I was reminded.

"Yeah, but I doubt anybody could break into this fortress," I replied, as I armed the security system.

An hour later, just as we pulled into the Fred Meyer parking lot, guess what?

"Hello?" I answered the shrill of the phone.

A recorded message informed me of our worse fears, the motion sensor had been set off, but listening, I could hear nothing unusual.

Later, we and the Tribal Police had a good laugh, and Bootsue spent the rest of the month locked up in the bedroom, whenever we were away. As I remember, the groceries had to wait until another day.

It was a comfortable, lazy summer, and we were again sorry to see folks come home. It was time for them to guard their own gold.

We were compensated with a nice bonus, a dinner and another great reference.

The creatures encountered at the Allen's were mostly larger critters, birds and mammals, but our next job introduced us to a variety of "smaller" creatures.

One thing was becoming very apparent...that is that the need for housesitters occurs in a ratio of over five to one; five times more in remote rural areas, than in urban. This formula was once again proven by the location of our next job; the furthest out yet, halfway between Pasco and Hanford. It was another mansion in a grove of trees, surrounded by dry sagebrush, with a nearby dairy, a breeding place for billions of flies.

It was an idylic pastoral place with a formal sunken English garden, overlooked by a three story tudor style home.

Petri & Gladys Optenheimer were middle-aged business people who ran their business from home, but had to travel a lot to their branch offices, which were located all over the Northwest.

They had a grown son somewhere, who was never to be admitted to their home.

"He's liable to try any sort of ruse to get a free bed," Gladys told us, "But you are not to allow him access under any circumstances."

"We'll be back in 11 days," added Petri, "Good luck!"

Bootsue had not lived in the same house with a cat, since Fiesty died, 3 years earlier. Optenheimer's had a spoiled long hair Persian, who lived in the master bedroom. Miss Sulky was named Annie and came down stairs once a day for her gourmet dinner, and she didn't understand when Bootsue only wanted to play.

We seldom saw Annie except when she took to prowling the house in the middle of the night after we were all asleep.

Bootsue, however, knew her every move, and would sneak out into the hallway, hide around a corner and lie in wait. It was usually around that witching hour of 2:00 am, when the fur would fly and the chase would be on.

Between pow-wow drums, woodpeckers, and midnight cat fights, we were soon becoming acclimated to these sudden night awakenings.

Part of their daylight basement had been converted to a bomb shelter during the scares of the "cold war". There were two concrete bunkers with concrete walls over two feet thick. Access to one was by way of the garden, and was home to many black widow spiders and or rats. Another was through the basement, with nothing but a flimsy glass door to the garden. There was no security system or alarms. And Del got to imagining this to be a good place for a wayward son to hide. Every little creak or sound, would send me down to investigate.

Another secret of this great house, was what we called the "Anne Frank room". A well hidden two foot square door was located in the back wall of a spare bedroom clothes closet. The surprise was that it opened into a full sized room.

In it there was a standard double bed and toy chest. The walls were finished and the small gabled window had curtains. Don't ask me how the bed was fitted through the two by two trapdoor…? This was another hiding place we had to frequently check to be sure the wayward son had not snuck in.

Between Bootsue, Annie and all the secret hidey-holes, our night life was still somewhat fearful.

But, that's not the end of the story...not yet!

Except for a few quail, we saw no wildlife at all, except for the insects. When the wind was just right, clouds of flies would blow up from the dairy, three miles away. The little buggers have always had a secret way of getting inside, which still remains one of life's deep secrets.

Fortunately, there was a "mud room" where we entered first, then sprayed insect killer, waited for two or three minutes, like in an airlock, then entered the main house. I'm sure the vapors we breathed in were harmful to our health.

This mud room was also the home of Elly, a very old Golden Retriever with a bladder problem. Poor Elly had not been able to hold her water, due to some disease from puppyhood. She was a sweet dog, but never allowed beyond the mud room. She had three blankets to sleep on, one of which had to be laundered every day. And the room's floor required frequent mopping, sometimes three or four times a day.

Elly would go hiking with me up in the sagebrush hills behind the house. She knew every trail. I did lots of hiking throughout all of our housesitting adventures, and one day witnessed a gang-style murder, requiring a winter return to testify in court. But that's another chapter.

Al Allaway

In additon to all the flies, there was a seasonal hatch of some little white moth just before we left the Optenheimer's. Whenever we forgot to close the car windows, we'd accumulate various insects. These moths had a liking for the car interior, and we had a devil of a time getting rid of them.

The next Sunday, Del and I walked into our church, as was customary, and just as I sat down, five or six of these moths exited from my coat pocket and decided to do an aerial display, as they made their way upward to the cathedral ceiling. It was difficult to ignore the snickers and whispers which we heard from behind us.

The sermon that morning had to do with "Not jumping to conclusions".

Snowbirds Guarding the Gold
RV Life & House-Sitting Adventures

Chapter Eight: "Murder, He Wrote"

(Psalm 23:4: "Yea, though I walk through the valley of the shadow of death, I will fear no evil: for thou art with me...")

The Yakima River Canyon between Selah and Ellensburg Washington is a pristine and scenic "national treasure". A winding two lane road twists up one side of the steep canyon while the Burlington Northern clutters the other.

Sheer basaltic rock cliffs tower up to a thousand feet above the river bed. The area is home to large and beautiful wildlife, the Mountain Sheep **(*Ovis canadensis*)**, Rocky Mtn. Elk **(*Cervus canadensis*)**, White-tail Deer **(*Odocoileus* *virginianus)*, and both Bald and Golden Eagles **(Haliaeetus leucocephalus** and **Aquita chrysaetos)**.

The river itself is a world-class trout stream; fly casting, catch and release only. Most fishing is accomplished by drift boat assisted by paid river guides. But in some of the areas where the canyon widens, numerous trails have been created by many years of hopeful trout sportsmen.

Except for an occasional rattlesnake or striped skunk, the 30-mile long canyon is devoid of much other small ground-living creatures. Few squirrels, fewer rabbits and no mice are ever visible. The reason for this is immediately apparent, as the canyon is overrun with abandoned pets; dogs, feral cats and even an occasional Vietnamese pot-bellied pig.

Like a green thread winding through desert mountains, the Yakima River Canyon attracts a bountiful botanical collection, in addition to all the wildlife. Euel Gibbons wrote a popular book in the 1960's titled *"Stalking the Wild Asparagus"* which was a survivalist guide to various nourishing wild plants and where to locate them. Perhaps he was thinking of just such an area as this lush river bottom land.

One canyon wide spot is quite large, perhaps 300 acres heavily timbered at about milepost 8.5 on State Route 821. The Department of Fish and Game has identified the driveway into the area as "Day-use only" fishing access. Directly across the highway is another driveway, leading uphill to half a dozen rich people's houses, including Phil and Steve Mahre, 1984 Olympic downhill skiing gold medal holders.

I've always been an outdoorsman, especially where there is a variety of flora and fauna to observe and classify before preservation by photography.

Thus it was during all four years of Yakima area housesitting that I had discovered this place and spent numerous hours in the wild, hiking, swimming, birding and stalking the lost sunshine of Arizona.

One spring, about the 2nd year or so, I discovered quite a few patches of *Asparagus officianale*, lush, crisp, tender wild asparagus. Lip-smacking, yummy, good!

Asparagus is not easy to find, because it is well camouflaged and so very difficult to see. It is only edible in mid spring when the new stalks are a foot or less in height, hidden amongst grasses and other plant shoots.

Unharvested spears, allowed to grow, will mature into feathery giant ferns, the female bearing bright red berries. At this stage, usually mid-summer, they stand out and are visible from many yards distance.

The trick, then, was to map the plants in summer, so you could remember where to look at harvest time the following spring. You couldn't be too obvious about this, because if you stuck a brightly colored stake or flag to mark each plant, you'd better believe it would attract others who were also looking for free food. And I was not in a mood to share this limited treasure.

Thus it was on a warm August day[1], with my mouth watering in anticipation for next spring's asparagus, I arrived on the river with a fistful of numbered wooden stakes, small enough to identify the location of a yummy asparagus plant, with only the top inch of the stake showing.

While I was sketching out a rough map and working about halfway between the river and 100 yards or so from the highway, the peace and serenity of a beautiful summer's day was suddenly shattered…

Did I imagine that the songbirds, who had long since accepted me as part of their landscape, suddenly grew quiet? The hush was immediately noticeable, and I looked up, to see three young men in close order, stumbling rapidly down the steep highway embankment. They disappeared into thick brush, and with a shrug, I returned my attention to the asparagus. I briefly wondered what they could be doing, so markedly out of place!

I did not wonder for long, because within 15 to 20 seconds, shots rang out, a rapid burst of semi-automatic gunfire, maybe 9-10 rounds.

---

[1] August 18th, 1999

The time was approximately 3:10 PM and time stood frozen, with slow motion images etching themselves into my brain...Permanently etching...this unwanted trauma.

My first thought was that those idiots were target-shooting, unaware of other people in the area. I almost stood up and hollered a warning like.

"Hey! Knock if off; there are people over here."

But, before I could gather enough sense to decide, two of them were scrambling back up the bank to the road. It was then that I noticed a small white car partly hidden behind some trees. As the two men reached the vehicle, I heard voices in distress and a car door slam.

Now, I started to feel a little uneasy, watching for the third guy, when suddenly, one of the first two started back down into the brush again. He then fired one final shot (the coupe de grace), ran back up the bank, jumped into the car which then sped off...

Suddenly, the day was no longer so sunny and bright; suddenly there seemed to be a weight of undefined responsibility thrust like a yoke about my neck. Suddenly, all interest in asparagus was lost; suddenly I felt a wave of confusion, followed by a wave of nausea...

Not a cricket, not a locust, no birds chirping; bees and flies were still. All Nature seemed to pause in horror and disgust. The only sound was of my own pulse, roaring in my ears.

There was no panic, not yet. Adrenaline and fear perhaps.

"What have I just witnessed?"

"Was it real, or only imagined?"

"Can I, in all conscience, just ignore all this and go home?"

"What if…?

"What if that man really got shot, and needed help?" I was not even sure where he was, perhaps he had walked out another way, unseen…?

Wishful thinking, and I knew it!

Groping for courage, I gathered my strength and began probing the dense brush along side the highway. Cautious, not to disturb a possible crime scene, I approached three likely spots, calling out, but knowing there would be no answer. Poison oak and thick stands of wild thorny roses prevented my penetration into the brush, as deep as I wanted to go.

"I'll be able to see more from the highway," I told myself, "Because I could look down into this tangle."

So back to my car I went, dumped my asparagus stakes, and drove around toward the main road where I stopped briefly to talk with some near nude sunbathers.

"Did you hear those shots ten or fifteen minutes ago?" I asked.

"We thought it was kids with fire crackers," replied a red-faced young man, quickly wrapping himself in a towel. His lady was hiding in the bushes.

"Well, it wasn't fire crackers," I informed them, "I saw guys shooting, and one of them is missing. I'm headed up to the highway to check it out."

From the highway, looking down, it didn't take long to locate a hand, part of a leg with tennis shoe sticking out of the brush. Closer examination revealed blood and gore. No doubt about it now.

Waving down the first several cars, two of which had cell phones, I hastily explained my need, but because of the canyon depth, they couldn't get a call out. A couple of ladies then volunteered to drove out to get help.

They soon returned and advised me that they had been able to reach 911 a short ways down the canyon and that police were on the way.

"You're shaking pretty bad," one of them told me, "Do you mind if we stay here with you until the police arrive?"

And so began the saga[2] of a drug deal gone sour and the cold blooded murder of one Carlos Bautista by his "friends" and contemporaries, all of whom were Hispanics living in Yakima and Selah.

It seemed hours before any real help arrived. The two ladies, a phone company man and I tried to protect the road shoulder around the scene from all the other curious drivers who tried to pull off and park, to find out what was going on.

---

[2] As reported in the *Yakima Herald-Republic*

The first deputy sheriff to arrive from Kittitas County was really skeptical, acting bothered and disinterested.

"What's the big fuss?" he chided, "There's corpses of dead deer down here lot's of times."

"Dead deer, indeed," I thought, "You'll be sorry, jerk!"

His demeanor changed drastically when I showed him the body, and it wasn't long after that, the area was swarming with cops and bright yellow "crime scene" ribbons. The Assistant District Attorney from Ellensburg even showed up.

It was perhaps three hours later when they released me to go home. My butt felt bruised from sitting on the hard plastic seat in the back of the police cruiser. Those things are not meant for comfort, and when I needed to get out, the officer had to release the door lock from up front. I was virtually held prisoner while they took my statements.

We were staying at the Penoyar's during this incident, and the real impact (shock) of it did not really hit me until after I arrived back home. I had tried to get the cops to pass the word on to Del, that I would be late, so she wouldn't worry, but they said their radio couldn't get out of the canyon.

Numerous additional visits with detectives were required at the scene, to establish my line of sight, distances and other evidence. It was most unusual that a witness would assist police in limited data gathering, but my crime scene savvy as a big city arson investigator may have influenced them.

My description of the suspects and their escape vehicle did reflect in a positive way in this investigation, and partially assisted in the apprehension of the two suspects three days later.

It goes without saying, that except for requests from the police, visits to this favorite nature retreat came to an abrupt halt for this season. I never did finish staking and mapping those asparagus. The area became tarnished and lost all it's attraction and luster for at least a year.

E-mail exchanges with the Sheriff's Office were humorously captioned, "More Spare Grass".

This writer finds it difficult to inject any humor into the writing of this chapter, but read on...the mood changes again in Chapter Nine, where we really did have to "Guard the Gold".

But, let's finish the murder saga first.

Having returned south to Yuma the 1st of October, I now received four different supoenas to appear for trial, which was set, postponed, then reset. The legal maneuvering kinda' kept our life unbalanced until the trial was finally settled to begin on December 13th. The county paid for round trip air fare, lodging and meals.

The trial was grueling, the defense questioning everything I said, crossing every "T" and dotting every "I".

A Refugio Camacho had been charged with first degree murder and was the only one on trial, as the other perp named

Raul Brambila, a juvenile, had plead guilty and was already serving a five year sentence.

Sitting in that Ellensburg courtroom for three days was like watching a legal drama unfold on the television, except that everything was vague, like in a foggy dream, and in slow motion. The benches were harder and more uncomfortable than the back seat of that police car.

The only highlight of the experience was Kittitas County's Victim/Witness Assistant, a sweet Christian lady named Adrianne Gerlach. Her kindness and consideration was the only bright spot of the whole trial. We have remained close e-mail buddies, ever since.

I was dismissed before the defense was heard and before the closing arguments. What I report following was gleaned from the newspapers...

The next day, a girl friend told the jury that Camacho had told her that he shot Bautista 10 or 11 times, and once in the head[3]. She continued, "It seemed to me he wanted someone to talk to about the murder, and told me he was worried about evidence he may have left behind. He said he was going to change the tires on his car and get rid of his shoes."

You're not going to believe the verdict!

So, Who dunnit? Is Justice blind? Or did Camacho have a good defense lawyer?

---

[3] Kittitas County *Daily Record,* December 16, 1999.

Remember, I saw *three* men come down and *two* go up, then *one* return and the *same one* leave. Also remember that the first burst of shots were so close together, they could have been from an automatic gun, and the last single shot was perhaps a minute or more *after.*

Closing remarks by the defense on the following Tuesday[4] as recorded in the newspapers, told jurors a totally different account of the day of the murder.

He said that a fourth man was hiding in the bushes when Bautista and Brambila got into a fight. Then Camacho supposedly fired a warning shot to break it up, dropped his gun to the ground to physically separate the two assailants, when this unknown fourth person grabbed Camacho's gun and shot Bautista.

And the stupid dumb jury bought it!...Camacho was "Innocent!"

I know justice was miscarried. I was too close, not to have heard a single "warning shot" before the main burst. The scenario used for the defense would have taken several seconds between the first shot, to drop the gun, to pick it up, then to take aim and to start shooting. The time lapse between the 1st and 2nd shots was *less than half a second!* I know, because I was there.

---

[4] As recorded in the *Yakima Herald-Republic,* December 22nd.

The other bold-faced lie has to do with the "fourth man", who if he continued to hide after the car drove off, would certainly have attacked me, who by this time would be most visible as an obvious witness to murder.

Camacho got off scott-free, except that he was deported back to someplace in Mexico by Immigration and Naturalization, as an illegal alien!

Believe me, we watched our back trail for many months after I returned to Yuma. Yuma, you know is only 10 miles from the Mexican border and there were over 50 Camachos listed in the Yuma county telephone directory!

Not all was lost, however. I've staked over 40 more asparagus plants during the following summers, and poor young Carlos Bautista fades further with each passing year, into the dim recesses of memory. Roadside flowers and a cross, placed by family, marked the spot for several months.

But Satan's fires will getcha' in the end, all you criminals who think you've escaped justice with your fancy lies, and sadly, you're gonna wish you had listened to your good momma!

(Romans 6:23 "For the wages of sin is death; but the gift of God is eternal life through Jesus Christ our Lord.")

Snowbirds Guarding the Gold
RV Life & House-Sitting Adventures

Part III,
"Going For the Gold"

The Goldberg "Castle"

Al Allaway

Chapter Nine: "Guarding the Gold Burg"

(Matthew 18:3 Verily I say unto you, except ye…become as little children, ye shall not enter into the kingdom of heaven.")

The long anticipated Millenium had finally crept in the backdoor, and all the fears of "Y2K" were behind us. We had our home in Yuma up for sale and were hoping to

Al Allaway

settle full time in the Yakima Valley. This would likely be our last summer housesitting, but believe me, would turn out to be the most memorable, if not the most humorous.

Last Fall, before we headed south, someone else placed an ad under Housesitters:

> **WANTED:** Retired couple to sit large house in exchange for light garden work. Call 000-0000.

This was not something we could possibly ignore, so we called the number, and a lady with an Oriental accent, barely speaking English, told us that they were to be gone overseas for long periods making motion picture films, and they needed full-time housesitters.

"Can you come right out?" she asked in broken English.

"Well, not really," I replied, "We spend the winters in Arizona, and only housesit in the summertime."

"Dang!" she said, "Call back in the springtime, then because we'll probably still need you. We have such a terrible turnover with our housesitters!"

"Is this telling me something?" I thought, as I took down the address and promised to contact her in the spring. She said her name was Millie Goldberg and they lived up the Naches River canyon, out past the sleepy little town of Nile.

"Goldberg?" I pondered, "Dang funny name for a Oriental, which I assumed to be Chinese."

I didn't know it yet, but here was the glimmering of an idea to write this book, all about this one job experience. But wait, I'm getting ahead of myself. The job won't start until sometime in the spring of 2000.

We wrote in March, telling the Goldbergs that we planned to arrive back in Yakima in time for Del's mom's birthday on the first of April, and asked if the job was still open.

A Mr. Fritz Goldberg wrote back, indicating that it was still open and that they were doing a lot of remodeling, like sanding hardwood floors, and could we wait an extra week before moving in? I wrote back, "No problem, we'll stay with Cousin Johnny again and telephone you when we get into town."

"Odd!" I thought, "Chinese people with German and Jewish names."

We've housesat for Canadians and for American Indians. This could get interesting.

Arriving in Yakima as planned, we moved into Cousin John's place the same day John headed to California to welcome a new grandbaby. The timing couldn't have been better. We had to care again for their dear little half blind and deaf poodle, Bogey.

On the second day, we called the Goldberg family to arrange for our first meeting.

"Anytime," Fritz said, "Just come on out…today vude be gutt"

We drove the 25 miles, following their directions to a cluster of seven mailboxes at the junction of the highway with a steep, poorly graded gravel driveway.

"Must be one of the houses on the top of this hill," I casually remarked to Del.

Her sixth-sense was whispering foreboding doubts, so thoughts and fears of trepidation were beginning to assail her.

"Are you sure that we want to spend the whole summer away out here?" she said, "I'm already fearful."

"Let's give it a chance," I replied as we started up the steep twisting driveway, "But, I sure wouldn't want to have to drive out here in the icy wintertime."

The first four houses bore nametags at their driveway junctions. The next one didn't, and was protected by a huge closed cattle gate. Through the gate, we could see two small private ponds and a huge castle-like stone house.

"That may be it," I said, "They told me it was the fifth driveway. But, let's go on up and look at the next house first."

The next "house" was a dilapidated old travel trailer with five or more huge dogs running free. The minute they saw us, they were all over our car, barking fiercely and scratching the car with their muddy paws.

"Not here," I said, hopefully. "Let's go back down to the stone castle."

There being no call-box at the gate, we drove on in, closing the gate behind us. More barking dogs, but seemingly more friendly. The driveway wound past one of the ponds, then entered a steep stone-walled courtyard. Once there, a second house was visible just as we found a place to park.

"Ah, yes," I remarked, "That must be the guest house they told me we're supposed to live in...I forgot to tell you."

"I ain't living in that!" Del snapped, "There's no glass in the windows." It was then that I noticed she was right, as a scruffy looking black cat jumped out through the opening.

"Spooky," I agreed, feeling the first urge to leave.

"Let's see if we can find a front door," I continued, "Fritz and Millie Goldburg should be expecting us."

The first door seemed to be a basement, with a door hanging on only one hinge, unfinished walls visible beyond, and construction trash laying all about.

The next door we found was an obvious "formal" front door entry, but barricaded and with wet cement visible. The doorbell wires were hanging out of their junction box in a haphazard design.

"Let's try around back," I suggested in desperation, "I can hear someone pounding."

"Be careful, don't step on those nails," Del warned.

We encountered someone, at last. He was a very short, barefoot Chinese man of about 65. When he opened his mouth to speak, it was with obvious German accent.

Trying to maintain control with dignity, I opened with, "You must be Fritz," as I offered my hand.

"We are Al and Del Allaway...about the housesitting job?"

"Ach, you ver supposed to come tomorrow, mine vife is in town chopping for groceries."

I resisted reminding him that two hours earlier he had told me, "Today is good...". Instead, I asked, "Can we look around, anyway?"

"Ja, okay, I guess...but ve're not going to need you yet for at least anoder veek."

Now, I'm beginning to wonder, if this is the same Fritz I had talked to earlier, but again resisted asking. This was becoming so weird!

He showed us his "castle", all three floors and all ten bedrooms, with a large indoor swimming pool in the daylight basement. It was indeed a mansion, as one would expect to see on the TV show, *Life Styles of the Rich and Famous.*"

But, construction clutter was everywhere and I couldn't help asking about it.

"I'm going to eventually make it into a bed and breakfast for all the hunters and fishermen who come to these mountains", he told us, "And, skiing is not so far off in the vintertime."

Fritz Goldberg wore a torn and very dirty sweatshirt unmatched with a pair of faded Bermuda shorts. His once black hair was extra long and wind blown. A carpenter's belt full of tools was attached around his overly chubby waist. He wore no hat and it was difficult to tell if the grey was natural hair, or filthy with cement dust. His smile was the only bright part of his otherwise grimy face.

He paused for a huge beer-belch. Then he answered Del's burning concern, "You'll have these two rooms and private bath, right here behind the kitchen."

Well, that, at least, caused a sigh of relief.

All we would have to do was to maintain a courtyard garden, a small vegetable garden and keep the pool clean, he told us.

"Can't be too many unexpected surprises, can there?" I asked Del, as we drove back to town. "Tomorrow, we'll come out again and meet Millie, and we'll bring Bootsue to see how she will get along with all these big dogs."

"How many were there?" she asked.

"Dunno," I replied, "We'll count them tomorrow."

So went the first interview, and we were looking forward to the next day, hoping to overcome some of the many many remaining doubts.

Next day, we got an early start, thinking to arrive too early for any of the principals to slip away. Arriving about two hours before the appointed time, we were met in the courtyard by a beaming Fritz, who was obviously trying to reverse any bad first impressions he had left with us the day before. His jet-black hair was combed and he wore much cleaner clothes. Behind him was a very young Chinese girl, openly nursing a fat little boy who had to be almost 2.

"Looks like some grandchildren are here today," said Del, before we got out of the car.

"More like great-grandchildren," I responded.

Fritz greeted us with a huge smile, as Bootsue barked a questioning "hello".

"Meet mine *kleinchen*, mine little vife, Millie, and mine son, Juan". We learned Millie was 21, and Juan was 18 months.

"How International," my thoughts repeated, A Chinese-German-Jew with a Spanish named son…"

Millie stepped forward, yanking Juan from her tit, and welcomed us in a very broken Chinese accent. Most women would have been blushing as the blouse was pulled over the exposed breast, but Millie seemed indifferent to any such protocol. Unbelievably, she turned out to be the same "mature" woman I had spoken with the previous year.

Bootsue was introduced to the three dogs, Zoe, Philly and Angel, all who seemed to accept her, after the traditional butt-sniff.

Going inside, we met Rosy, the weekday housekeeper-cook. Rosy had a mouth like a sailor, which spewed forth truck-driver obscenities every time she opened it.

"Great verbal contrasts!" I thought.

The kitchen-living-entry room of this home was a vaulted-ceiling of almost 25 feet height, showing huge timbers. The two outside walls were of blue tempered double-paned glass, each piece over eight feet in both dimensions. The second floor balcony, like a mezzanine, overlooked the slabs of black marble which served as a floor. The room's three main decorations were a potted *Cylindropuntia* cactus over 20 feet tall nearly touching the ceiling, an ebony grand piano which matched the marble floors, and what appeared to be a three ton solid jade full sized tiger statue, heavy enough to sink through the floor.

Fritz, Millie, Del and I were seated at a huge plank like table, reminding one of King Arthur's medieval dining hall. It could easily have served 20 people.

"Let's agree on a few basics", I started the interview, still trying to maintain control, "Like keys, security systems, well pumps, fire protection and so-on." Rosy snickered in the background.

"Your job von't be to vorry about stuff like dat," Fritz explained, "Besides, ve don't ever use any keys."

"When are you leaving?" Del asked.

Fritz explained that they owned houses in Seattle, Hawaii and in Hong Kong, besides this one, and they would be "in and out" all summer, following no particular schedule.

"I also haf a two month contract with Microsoft to make a film all over Asia, sometime this summer," Fritz continued, "So ve vant you to be here, even ven ve are in residence."

"Without keys or locks, what happens when we have to leave, like for Church or shopping?" I queried.

"Not to vorry," Fritz replied, "Just try to go ven the other housesitter is here."

"Other house-sitter?"

"Yes, Victor. He lives upstairs!"

Del and I shot secret glances at each other, and wondered what kind of a circus we were getting ourselves into.

Fritz said he had to get back to the floor sanding and that he would call us when he got the floors sealed in six days, then we could move in.

"Perfect," I thought, Cousin John will be coming home from California in six days.

But, did we really want to take a chance in this obvious insane asylum? Time would tell.

Chapter Ten: "Settling-Into the Asylum"

(Psalm 139:16 "Your eyes saw my unformed body (in my mother's womb). All the days ordained for me were written in your book before one of them came to be." NIV)

Six days later, Cousin John had not yet come home, so I called Fritz and Millie Goldberg, to find out how things were progressing.

"The floor sealer has to dry another few days," he said, "Bring some things out, if you need to, but you can't move in yet."

"How many days are a 'few'?" I was getting tense.

"Oh, give it at least another veek."

"Ratz..." I said to Del, hanging up the phone, "We're homeless for at least another week! What idiodic stress!"

Just then the phone rang.

"Hello?" I answered, secretly hoping Fritz had reconsidered. No such luck...It was Cousin Johnny.

But, talk about God's great timing...John wondered if we might be able to stay on for another week or so, to which we readily agreed.

Allelulia!

During the next week, we made several more excursions to the Goldberg's property, becoming more and more familiar with what was to be our summer long home. Each trip included some of our linens, canned goods and the computer. The room Fritz had assigned as our bedroom, had a second phone line for Internet hookup, but still no furniture.

The closet shelves and window sills were still covered with a half inch of fine sanding dust. Only the floors were "clean", and gooey wet with a slow drying sealant...still too wet to walk on.

We met Victor on one of these trips, and we thought we had found a reliable ally. At least he was someone we could talk with after the Goldbergs left (If they ever did). And he could share important information with us without obscenities like Rosy.

It was at least two more weeks before we finally moved in, almost a month late. It was the 1st of May. Cousin Johnny had finally come home, and we had spent an extra week in a motel.

Our bedroom was large and roomy, 16 feet by about 20. One whole wall was made with those same 8 foot square blue tempered glass panels as in the front room. But there were no drapes, and the late afternoon sun heated the room to unbearable temperatures. These huge blue panes were permanent, with no way to open them for ventilation. I understood that they had cost somewhere over $1000.00 each.

Del had just concluded another surgery, removal of a cyst under a knee cap, and was back on crutches, so in addition to the queen size bed, they provided her with a rocking chair and an electric fan, the only furniture outside of an old typing table which held my computer. I brought my own 6 ft. folding table, and castered office chair. The chair brought an instant frown from Fritz, who claimed it would mark up his expensive new floor. So, I bought a plastic office floor mat to protect it.

The only window in the room was of the wind-open type which opened not to the outside, but into a hallway, not the same hallway we used for access into the room. This other hall ran through a new part of the house, still under construction.

One end was at the hanging door I had earlier described as looking like a basement, so the whole hallway was open to the outside, the other end opening onto a balcony which ran all along the big blue window-wall. Anybody walking in either place could look fully into our bedroom.

When we were settled in, we had several requests of Fritz.

"How about some drapes for the window wall?" I started.

"Ve haf ordered," answered Fritz.

"Television?" I asked.

"Bring vun over from Seattle house, next time ve go."

"When do you plan to leave us?" Del asked.

"Tomorrow ve go to Seattle!"

Alright!

The next morning, Rosy arrived at 8:00 am, and we heard many men talking and laughing in the kitchen.

Peeking out the door, I saw Rosy serving coffee and breakfast to six burly construction types. After slipping on some clothes, I tip-toed out, so as not to wake Del.

"Good morning," I ventured. "Is Fritz up yet?"

"They left for three days". Rosy growled.

I hesitated, "Who are these guys?"

"Don'tcha know nuthin, stupid?" she said, "They're the [bleeep] construction workers."

"What workers?" I thought to myself, knowing better than to ask.

"Come up and see me, Al," called a voice from the mezzanine. It was Victor.

Upstairs, Victor sat me down for a "father-son" talk.

"You've gotta ignore loud-mouth down there," he whispered. "She hates men." He explained that nobody ever talks to Rosy before noon, and then only if the house is on fire.

He told me that the construction workers were here almost every weekday, helping Fritz rebuild. There was a rumor going around that the "remodeling project" had been going on for years, and it would never be finished. That was because some of the county building laws delay assessment of taxes on the value of new construction "until it is finished"…?

"I noticed fresh dog poop on the stairs on the way up here," I said, "What's that all about?"

"Oh, Fritz and Millie left about 3:00 am, and forgot to close the gate at the foot of the stairs. Those crazy dogs do that anytime they can get up here. If the choice was mine," he said, "I'd shoot 'em."

He further explained that Rosy refuses to clean up after the dogs, so he has to do it. Poor Victor!

When I went back downstairs, the workers were all done with their breakfast, so I tiptoed back into our room, so as not to wake up Del, but just then a table saw roared into life, in the hallway, just outside the open window. I'm glad I was there to ease her sudden awakening.

Bootsue, also startled, cut loose with a barrage of barking, as yet another worker strutted by on the veranda, outside the blue glass window.

So much for sleeping in on weekday mornings! And we'd have to find some spare bed sheets to tack up over the windows.

As I understood it, these guys were all on Fritz's payroll and I was yet to learn why they were so happy on this day when Fritz was absent.

My next encounter with Rosy was a little more friendly. I had to ask her how and where to turn on the lawn sprinklers.

"It's about time," she said, "I'm getting [blank.] tired of doing someone else's [bleep]..ing job."

She led me down a rickety spiral staircase to the daylight basement, into Millie's "office". Turning sharply down a narrow dimly lit hallway behind the stairs, we walked past shelves of motion picture film cans. The hallway turned 90 degrees and got narrower and darker, with one small bare light bulb burning 30 feet further down at the end.

If I was in a Count of Monte Cristo movie, I wondered where my hand held oil torch was…

"It's in there," she said, stopping at a tiny crawl hole, which was about two feet above the floor, "The water valve, I mean."

The hole was covered with a small plywood door about 2 feet square, certainly not big enough to admit a fat person.

"There's a light switch on the right side, just inside the hatch," she continued, "Then about twenty feet down the passageway, you'll find the [bleep]...ing valve just over your head."

"Will you stay here, while I look for it?" I cautiously asked.

"What'r'ya, a [bleep]...ing chicken?" she replied, "Okay, but just this once."

Creeping through the small opening, the crotch of my pants got caught on an unseen nail.

Rosy snickered. Working myself loose, I stood up on the other side.

"What's all this white powder on the ground?" I asked.

"That's lime," she answered, "Fritz spreads it around down here to discourage the [bleep] rattlesnakes."

Whoa!

The passageway was damp and narrow. I could hear water dripping somewhere. The wall on my right was the backside of the basement foundation. The floor was busted up rock of varying sizes, littered with occasional construction debris. The opposite left-hand wall was hewn out of solid rock, making the passage barely wide enough to walk through without scraping arms and shoulders on each side.

True enough, I found the valve right where she said and as I reached up over my head, Rosy shouted further instructions.

"Only turn the valve about 70 degrees, or you'll flood out the garden, she said, "And don't let it run for more than an hour."

Then she was gone, and I wasn't sure whether or not she had locked me in this dungeon. And dungeon it was; I'd have to crawl in here four times each week to turn the water on, and four more times to shut it off.

Later, I told Del about the "dungeon" and offered to show it to her, but because she was still on crutches, she couldn't yet get down the stairs. During the summer, we had several guests, including Del's mom, who all refused to even look.

"No snake-pits for me," they'd say.

The next day was Saturday and we thought we might be able to sleep in. But, at some early hour, Rosy had arrived to start her day.

We were awakened by a loud rhythmic thunk, thunk, thunk coming from the laundry room which was right next to our room. Once I was awake enough to recognize the disturbance, I assumed that it was from metal rivets banging in the dryer, rivets like the ones on coveralls, like Fritz and Juan both wore.

We put up with this racket for several days, until it finally became our turn to do laundry. I loaded the dryer with a load of wet clothes, and sure, enough, there it was again, thunk, thunk, thunk, and we didn't own any coveralls.

"Something wrong here," I told Del, "Let's check this out."

Sure that the noise was coming from inside the dryer drum, we unloaded all our clothes, and groped around in the bottom of the dryer.

"Peach pits," I exclaimed, "Six of them!"

It seems that little Juan had found a place to hide his treasures.

Doing laundry was always a hassle because Rosy had "priority" every weekday morning. And Millie or Fritz could start a load anytime it occurred to them. Victor and Del and I often had to wait until after dark or some other inconvenient time.

Other than our private bath, this laundry room also contained the only other restroom on this floor. The door was often closed, with the room in use by one of the construction workers.

The laundry caused another inconvenience. Any minor drop in water pressure would cause a pump somewhere to kick in, so the pressure would be up and down like a yo-yo. And we could almost guarantee that someone else would draw water the minute we got our shower adjusted. Most of the time the shower would run quite cold, there being no modern mixer valves to regulate pressure or temperature.

"If this was a bed and breakfast," I told Del, "Nobody would ever come back!"

"Look on the good side," she reminded me, "At least the swimming pool is warm."

Goldberg was proud of his many fruit trees, mostly peaches and Bosque pears. My "dungeon" rainbirds watered some of them, but most had to be watered by hand. He also insisted that the lawn be mowed at least twice a week, so I was usually busy doing chores two to three hours each day.

There was a walkway which Del could manouver with her crutches through the courtyard garden, which wound down to the daylight basement which had two entrances, one into Millie's office and the other into the large room where the swimming pool was. This was the only way she could access the pool. It was heated and large enough for lap swimming, ranging in depth from 3 feet to 8 feet.

The pH and chlorine balancing was Millie's job, so all I had to do was keep the pool clean, full and covered. This covering turned out to be a major job, because of all the dust and trash of construction. Even with the cover, and nobody using it, the pool bottom was filthy and had to be vacuumed almost daily. Once I saw baby Juan spooning dirt from a potted palm into the pool.

"Aha," I thought, "So he's the culprit!"

Eighteen month old Juan, at the edge of this deep pool with no parent nearby, was a disaster looking for a place to happen. I scooped up Juan and took him bawling to his father.

Fritz couldn't understand why I was so upset.

"If he falls in the water, he'll learn to be more cautious," he said with a shrug. "Leave him alone." I would soon learn that this strange child rearing method would continue to raise it's ugly head.

Juan was large for his age, and very friendly. He followed his daddy everywhere, barefoot in heavy construction; barefoot because daddy was too. They'd step on nails and concrete chips as if they were feathers. Dents existed all over the property, where Juan imitated daddys action with a hammer. Fritz didn't seem to mind Juan lugging man sized tools anywhere on the property, again using the philosophy:

"If he hurts himself, he'll be more careful next time!"

"If he lives long enough," I thought to myself.

Unbelievable! Even when Juan ran a staple through Fritz's foot from an electric staple gun, nothing changed.

Baby Juan, now 19 months old, took a shine to Del, and spent hours in our room. The trouble was, he tugged off his diaper and ran around naked a lot and eliminated body wastes wherever and whenever it pleased him.

After he pooped on our only throw rug, we had to restrict him from our room for this most obvious reason.

He really became such a nuisance that we had to go to town to buy a lockset to replace the doorknob to our room. He was very upset with us for awhile after that. But, later, whenever we would come into the house, he'd run up to Del, giving her a big hug, and calling out, "Oma, oma!" Which is German for grandmother.

He also spoke some Chinese and was learning English, too. Poor little Juan, well advanced in speech and physical development, but so far behind in other things. Whenever he saw his mom, he'd run up, as if to hug her too, but instead would dive for her blouse, and have it pulled up before anybody could stop him. She had gone dry, she said, but baby Juan still had a nipple fixation.

Early on, we noticed that Juan had no regular toys to play with, only daddy's tools and some kitchen utensils. After several trips to a second-hand store, we managed to find some toy trucks and balls, which he loved. Fritz never did thank us.

The view from the veranda outside our bedroom was spectacular; we could see three distant timbered ridges and valleys in several directions. Most attractive was the Tieton River threading its way along, hundreds of feet below us.

On warm days, especially weekends, there would be hundreds of bright splashes of color, floating eastward, down the cascading rapids. It reminded me of a Walt Disney *Fantasia* scene of hundreds of brightly colored leaves; golden, reds, orange, purple and brown, floating lazily on a gentle brook. But binocular disclosure revealed a much more active scene; large and small rafts and kyacks ridden by people in brightly colored wet suits.

Standing on the veranda, we often saw Mountain sheep, elk, deer and occasionally a bear.

Millie was not good at delivering (or understanding) messages. And the housekeeper, Rosy could care less. We had lost calls even when we were there, simply because it was too much trouble to find us. Lots of things were bothering us, and we would have been out of there long ago if it wasn't free rent.

I had prepared a short list, to remind Fritz of some of his promises, and adding a few more:

Bathroom:

1. *No cosmetic-shaving light*
2. *Floor tile grout Huge loose pieces in shower hurt feet.*
3. *Broken parts of shower door frame (Have drawn blood, twice)*
4. *Replace missing shower door to stop water damage*
5. *Marble tiles falling off in shower*
6. *Provide means to control cold air*
7. *Provide source of heat*
8. *Stabilize sink and sink pedestal*

Large Bedroom:

1. *Provide curtains or drapes*
2. *Replace missing closet doors*
3. *Provide TV, and cable or satellite hookups*
4. *Electrical outlets will not hold the average plug*
5. *Repair or replace closet lighting system*

I gently suggested that these things would be required before he could ever consider opening a "bed and breakfast".

Al Allaway

We had been assigned one-half of one shelf in their large commercial size refrigerator, which we had to keep filled up, or lose. This was because Fritz kept his beer on the other half of our shelf, and the quantity was usually more than the shelf could hold.

There is a virtue called Patience, which is discussed many times in the Book of Proverbs. And, as this was certainly not a Christian home (It was Buddhist), we were still learning about Patience, better than in any Bible study.

Snowbirds Guarding the Gold
RV Life & House-Sitting Adventures

Chapter Eleven: "It's a Dog's Life!"

(Proverbs 20:1-2 "Wine is a mocker, strong drink is raging: and whosoever is deceived thereby is not wise. The fear of a king is as the

roaring lion: whoso provoketh him to anger sinneth against his own soul.")

Fritz said that he really loved his dogs. Philly and old Zoe had come with him from Hawaii.

These two were the good dogs, for the most part, and well behaved. Zoe slept on the living room sofa all day and would growl and resist if anyone tried to move her. She was pretty fierce for her fat old age. To get her to go outside, Victor told me to tip the leather sofa so her 70 pounds of blubber would just slide off onto the floor.

Philly was the only long hair and barked a lot and would nip at your heel at least once. Fritz told us that Philly was just expressing his love and acceptance of new people when he nipped their heels.

When we first moved in, their total dog count was three, rounded out by Angel. Misnamed, Angel was a boy dog, who talked to us and loved to have his belly rubbed. Fierce looking with pit-bull blood in him, Angel was a real contrast; a kid in a dog suit, with a big dog body, but the temperment of a toy Pekinese. Angel would also have been included with the "good dog" list, above, except nobody had ever bothered to house break him. It was usually Angel who did his thing in the upstairs hallway, much to Victor's disgust.

But let's not forget Baby, the gray cat. Baby was a tom and would often be gone for over a week at a time. Nobody seemed concerned. Baby was friendly enough, usually walking around on counter tops and food preparation areas. He was the alternate "housekeeper" working on Rosy's days off. Millie was a sloppy cook, but Baby licked up all her scraps. Baby often curled up to sleep in the middle of the "King Arthur" board table.

Nobody seemed offended, because even naked Juan walked on the dining table, helping himself to food from anybody else's convenient dinner plate.

By our second week, the dog count had risen to six...

The first stray to show up was Spot, a young stud Retriever who was as skinny as a rail. Spot learned how to lean on outer doors to open them. Spot and Angel hit it off right away, and soon found it necessary to start marking territory several times a day, INSIDE the house. The Grand piano was one of their favorite targets.

After their daily "rounds" started to include our bedroom door, I began to understand why Rosy, the housekeeper was such a grouch.

The 2nd stray was there only two days and then moved on.

Next was another bird dog with the same coloration as Spot, only female. She was named Mama, as her condition made it obvious that she had just nursed a large litter of pups somewhere.

Last in the line-up was a little girl black lab pup named Frankie.

So there were now six, who had to pee everyday to mark territory both inside and outside the house, and I was taking more notes with the idea of writing a book someday about all this, and thinking it's gonna' be a real ***humdinger!***

Poor Victor, the other house-sitter, now has to shovel dog poop out of the upstairs almost every day.

I had written up a list of chores, to avoid any misunderstandings with Fritz, who it turned out, had a horrible temper.

Carefully listing every job responsibility. I had skillfully skirted the dog feeding chore. When I wrote up the list, it said: **"Item 15: DOGS & CAT: Victor will feed weekends. Rosy, the rest of the week."** Nobody questioned this, and I thought perhaps I had won a small skirmish, while still losing the war.

Sometime in mid summer, Millie's cousin from Korea arrived for a visit. She was a little wisp of a thing, named Yoo, speaking no English at all. It turns out that she was fearful of all dogs, including our little Shih-tzu, Bootsue. She'd cringe in terror any time Bootsue's wagging tail crossed the room.

At this time, Fritz was away, alone, on a short trip, so to satisfy Yoo, all the doors were kept locked, with all of the dogs outside.

Fritz would have had a fit, but the nights were warm and the dogs didn't seem to mind at all. More than just latched, the doors had to be locked, because Spot had taught others how to stand up and push down on a lever to open doors. Remember, there were no keys, and the doorbell had not yet been wired together.

Del and I had gone shopping, and upon our return, we couldn't raise anybody to let us in, so had to gain entry through a back window because they couldn't hear us knocking.

Millie and Yoo were at home, and had locked all the doors just to satisfy Yoo's phobia.

Out in these hills, skunks were frequent visitors. One of the reasons for this was obvious. Fritz didn't believe in garbage service, instead, he kept digging trenches where household garbage was burned and buried. And this was a natural attraction to scavengers.

Being outside at night, it wasn't long before the dogs got hit by a skunk. We'd hear them howling in the night and smell the results. That settled to dog poop problem for awhile, at least until Fritz returned.

One morning, Rosy woke me with a knock on the door.

"They've killed a [bleep]...ing skunk and dragged the remains up onto the balcony," she complained, "And I don't do skunks! Take care of it, Al!"

Cautiously, trying not to gag, I moved the carcass down to the garbage trench, not thinking to also bury it.

And, sure enough, the next morning, there it was again, back on the veranda. Tail-wagging dogs stood off at a distance, waiting for my acceptance of their gift and watching to see what I'd do next. This time the skunk got buried under several hundred pounds of busted concrete blocks.

The skunk's mate got 'em all again the next night, and a big fight ensued. This time Millie and Rosy loaded them all in the station wagon for a trip to the vet, and anti-rabies shots.

Phew!

A week later, Frankie disappeared, and late that night, Fritz returned and we heard him verbally abusing Millie most of the night. (Their bedroom was right above ours).

The next morning, he lit into us with an unwarranted venomous anger. He accused us of losing his favorite dog. His anger was irrational and crazy. We went to our room, hoping he would cool off.

I sat down and composed the following letter:

Notes for letter which we hope we never have to share:

Dear Fritz: I'm sorry that you "lost" Frankie the black lab last night. I haven't the slightest idea what could have happened. All the dogs were here at about 9 or 9:30. They were all outside. We called Philly and Zoe inside. The other four were all playing "pack" and could care less whether they came inside or not. What you may or may not be aware of is that all the dogs, including Philly and Zoe spent most of the nights outside because of Yoo. Yoo was terribly fearful of all the dogs; she even cringed when little Bootsue was around. Her trauma was very real (although very unreasonable). All of us understood her terror of dogs. It is for that reason primarily that the south door was kept locked and at least two of the three east doors latched at all times. Spot and Mama (you've renamed her Lady) both learned how to stand up and press down to open the doors, so this was necessary.

So far as Frankie is concerned, I have a good guess what happened, one you're not going to like. I theorize that her owner came by sometime last night between 9:30 and midnight and that Frankie recognized that person (She has, you know been grieving, and looking over the wall a lot lately) and hopped into their vehicle. The dog, which was not yours in the first place, has probably been returned to its rightful owner.

Additional comments that I wish to make: 1) You offended me with two unwarranted personal attacks today. The first was when you said **"I've had a lot of sloppy housesitters, but you're the first one to lose a dog..."** *and then, later in the conversation:* **"You take a lot better care of your Boosoo that you do of my dogs."** *That's a ✡✓☺♣ lie and you know it! For both of these statements, you owe me a serious and sincere apology. 2) The second thing I want to say to you is this: If you "loved" your dogs so much and cared for them at all, why haven't you bought cheap collars for them with ID tags? Why haven't you built some kennels for them? Why haven't you taught them any obedience?*

Why do you let them in the house without housebreaking them first? Is it because you always have maids and servants to clean up the poop and pee? You must realize that dogs can be trained not to do this...Angel and Spot can be outside for hours, and within 5 minutes of letting them in the house, they make the rounds, squirting walls, doors and furniture in every room they can get access to. I've seen Angel pee on your expensive Grand piano on at least five occasions...but nobody cares! If we were so negligent of your dogs, Del would not have treated Spot when he cut his leg open, but of course you couldn't have known about that! So, please, the next time you feel like "flying off the handle" at everybody within shouting range, maybe you should learn some of the fact first.

The letter was never given to Fritz, because he did cool down and we had a good talk to clear the air.

Conflicts with Rosy and the kitchen were also cleared up. Drawers they had given us to use, were always filled with their stuff. And happened to be low enough so Juan could gain access. One day our only good teflon skillet was found out in the courtyard, filled with dirty sand. Juan was a busy little kid, totally unleashed and allowed to do whatever he pleased.

Our "sqeaky-wheel" complaints finally resulted in some minor charges. We were awarded a higher drawer. There was a different shelf in the oversize commercial refrigerator which was also assigned to us, but was still always full of Fritz's beer.

I swear, they went through two full cases (48 cans) of Budweiser every day. Millie and Yoo didn't drink any, and I never saw Rosy with one, so Fritz and his work crew were the drunks. Victor wouldn't dare drink in the daytime, because he worked afternoons for the County Corrections Division, in the Inmate Job Placement Dept.

Al Allaway

We ate out a lot, to avoid further conflicts in the kitchen. Another reason was that when Fritz was home, the dogs (All 6) were allowed inside, and if you sat at the big table for a meal, it was a foregone conclusion that a big wet dog nose would be resting on your lap, waiting for a tidbit. That is, if the cat or Juan didn't steal if off your plate first.

I think this is where our Bootsue learned to sit under the table, waiting for a scrap to fall. One thing good I can say is that all the animals were well fed…there were never any food fights, even with seven dogs and a cat in competition. The only real growling I remember was the daily ritual of getting Zoe to go outside before bedtime.

Item 6, on my "to-do chores" list had to do with mail pickup. **"MAIL: First up the driveway, pickup at box out on the main road. Attach mail for Victor under clothes pin at top of message board. Leave Goldberg mail on kitchen counter."** We had our mail coming to this address, so had to check it everyday, and were usually the only ones picking it up. Every month I noticed lots of mail, usually checks, to a person named Jen Wah Soo. One noticable envelope from an annuity payment department of a large insurance company, caught my attention, and I snuck a peek at the amount which was partially visible through the window in the envelope. It was for slightly over $50,000. and one just like it arrived every month. I knew that Fritz was a member of The Millionaires Club, but this raised my curiosity, especially as it was payment to either an alias, or someone who didn't live there.

One day I ventured, "When are you going to Asia on that Microsoft photo shoot?" I asked.

Millie jumped in, "Don't ask, they just fired him!" Fritz was too busy drinking another beer.

Then I thought it safe to ask, "What am I supposed to do with all this mail for Jen Wah Soo?"

"Oh, that's ours," she said, "Jen Wah Soo is his ex-wife…"

Oops! *Leave it alone, Al! It's none of your business!*

Rosy often accompanied Millie to town on shopping trips and we were told that Rosy was teaching Millie all about American customs, and money, and especially how to find the best bargains and get the most out of Cosco and Fred Meyer. Sometimes they'd stop for lunch and be gone for many hours.

Because Del was still lounging around on crutches, they just assumed that she'd babysit Juan.

"We'll only be gone an hour, or so," they said, "Would you mind watching the baby?"

"Well, I guess so," said Del, "But don't be long." I think that she was hoping Juan could get through the hour without needing mom's nipple.

They were gone five hours, and not even a "Thank you".

That night, Fritz got mad and lit into Millie again, and we wanted to cringe under our bed. He yelled and cursed so loud the walls shook. Poor Millie!

"We need to start thinking about getting out of here," Del said.

"Yeah," I answered, "I feel like I'm living in a doghouse."

And we were!

Thus began the "dog-days" of summer.

Chapter Twelve: "Domineering Domestic Relations"

(Nahum 1:3 "The LORD is slow to anger, and great in power, and will not at all acquit the wicked: the LORD hath his way in the whirlwind and in the storm, and the clouds are the dust of his feet.")

As the summer's "dog-days" stretched into early Fall, we were still there, and wondering why.

Fritz's anger was seething every morning, and drowned in beer by suppertime.

Six of his construction workers had been fired and replaced for minor misunderstandings. I thought that Fritz probably communicated with them like he did with me, leaving too much to be assumed. We'd gotten friendly with some of the "boys" and were sorry to see them gone. Fritz could never admit, that most of the problem was probably of his own making.

Millie was beside herself, wishing to return to Hong Kong, but he wouldn't allow it. She cried on Del's shoulder several times, and we learned that she never wanted to have Juan in the firstplace, and that he was an "accident". Now, we learned, that she was pregnant again, but <u>Don't tell Fritz.</u>

Del tried to talk her out of an abortion, but to no avail, so Millie and Yoo "went shopping" one day. Fritz was too drunk and never noticed, or questioned why they came home without any groceries.

We had repeatedly put this Buddhist family on our prayer lists, and we cried a lot for them.

Millie kept the books and payroll for Fritz's filming business, so she got a double dose of his wrath, one as wife and another as secretary.

Fritz's temper was getting more and more out of control and we began to worry about our own physical safety. When they argued in the room upstairs over our bedroom, we hoped the thumpings we heard were innocent, like foot stomping or such.

We did notice bruises on Millie, but she refused to talk about it.

We talked to Victor about it and he, of course, suggested that it's not our business and to keep out of it, but one couldn't help but feel a lot of pain for Millie...and then, what's young Juan learning from all this; to be abusive just like daddy? Poor kid!

We still had no drapes or TV. A bed sheet hung over the window in the hallway. None of the other requested repairs had been made, either.

One of the few Saturdays that we hoped to enjoy sleeping past 8:00 am, abruptly ended at 8:15 by the jangling of the telephone. It was Rosy.

"I'm not coming to work today," she growled, "They finally gave me a [bleep]..ing day off."

"Why tell me?" I asked.

"You'll have to feed them [blank] dogs," she replied.

"Okay, later," I said, hanging up the phone and falling back into bed...

Al Allaway

At 8:20, only five minutes later, the scratching started just outside our window, and that brought an immediate series of warning barks out of Bootsue.

"No sleep for the wicked," I told Del, "We gotta feed the dogs. Big mouth has the day off."

I'll never figure out how Angel and Spot figured out in only twenty minutes that we were their only ticket to breakfast.

Goldberg's had a 55 gallon drum filled with dry dogfood, so last night's left over table scraps were mixed with the Ol'Roy and some water, and the day was ours.

And a beautiful, bright sunny day it was too, so we decided to go for a drive and a picnic. The absence of Fritz's pickup was a fact we barely noticed.

Returning just about dusk, it was no surprise to find the house dark and quiet. Millie and Fritz often went to dinner and a movie, or perhaps out visiting friends.

All the doors were standing open, and the dog Philly was missing. Checking all around the house, we found nothing out of order except the missing dog. No one was home, so we called Rosy, who lived a couple of miles across the canyon.

"We just came home and found the doors all standing open," I explained, "And do you have any idea where Philly might be?"

Rosy was a little bothered with us calling her at home. "They always take Philly with them when they go to Seattle", she explained, "Is that the only [bleep] reason you are bothered me?"

"Well...?" says I, "And when did they go to Seattle?"

"Yesterday, you dumb [bleep], don't you know nuthin?"

"Are they coming back tonight?"

"No!"

"Thanks for your time, Rosy."

I turned to Del, "Did you see a note anywhere, telling us they were going to Seattle?"

"No," she said, "But we'd better look around a bit more."

Ten minutes later, the phone rang. It was Fritz. He was extremely upset, and very inebriated.

"Vat vas stolen?" he demanded, "Is my big jade tiger okay?"

It seems that Rosy had called them in Seattle and got him all shook up.

"Nothing's wrong here, Fritz," I explained, "When are you coming back?"

"Not for three days," he said, "Where've you been all day?"

"Why?"

"Vell, don't you think it better you stay home when ve are avay?"

"Sure," I replied, "But only when you share with us the fact that you are leaving..."

Long period of silence...

"Vell, you are sure notting is missing?"

"I'm sure."

The fool called back twice more before midnight, inquiring about the TV, then the VCR and silverware. And he was still worried about is jade tiger. Freight alone on it had cost him over $50,000 from China, he had earlier told us, but the statue weighed almost three tons...not something an ordinary thief could simply walk off with.

"I vant to file a police report next veek," he said, "You write a statement about everything you did and what you found, okay?"

"Sure," I agreed, all the time thinking, "What a jerk!"

"Perhaps I'll have to write a report for the Yakima County sheriff," I told Del, "It's best to write everything down while it's still fresh in our mind."

"Yeah," she said, "There's been no one here, but if he insists, then do it." So we outlined the following letter:

>   *To Whom It May Concern:*
>
>   *We are Rodney M. "Al" Allaway and wife, Delpha E. Allaway, currently living in the Fritz Goldberg residence at 270 Cliffdell View Drive, Nile, WA. We are here in the capacity of "House-sitters".*
>
>   *On Saturday, August 12th, 2000, between 1830 and 1900 (probably closer to 1900) we arrived "home" and were greeted by the dog "Angel". We entered through the east side foyer (of three doors). If I remember*

correctly, the outer door was stuck in a way that would have been caused by a hard slam (the wind was blowing very strong). The middle and inner doors were both standing open a few inches. Dogs "Spot" and "Zoe" were inside the house and greeted us with the usual. I then noticed the south (kitchen) door standing wide open, but thought nothing of it, because these dogs have learned how to open doors. The fourth dog, "Lady" was nowhere to be seen.

Within a few minutes of our arrival, the owners called from Seattle and expressed concern about missing dogs and/or stolen or missing items from the house. They had not informed us that they were leaving, so we were not even aware they had left the county. We searched around and finally found all the dogs, and assured the owners that there was nothing that appeared to be out of order.

Written and signed 1530 on Sunday, August 13th, 2000

We gave the letter to Fritz, and never heard any more about it. It was no surprise when the Sheriff never showed up to take a report.

It was now September, and we were still there..."waiting for the other shoe to fall".

Fritz has had some terrible bouts with his temper, and we all cringed when he was on the warpath. Poor Millie…if she was not physically abused (I've seen bruises) she certainly was mentally abused.

Some nights it appeared so violent that we were prepared to flee. I had nightmares of witnessing yet another murder, and long hours of interrogation, and glances implying guilt, as if I could have done something to prevent a tragedy. As long as Millie refused to sign a complaint, there was nothing we could do, except involve them in our prayers.

Domestic relations of this type are becoming more and more common in today's world. Much of it is related to ethnic background. In many societies, woman is still considered to be subservient.

The Lakota Sioux are said to have solved this inequity many years ago in a folklore tale, called "Woman of the Teepee" in which the mighty warrior is made to realize the value of his Lmuma[1] (woman, wife) without which, he would be a "skinny, naked man".

In our eyes, then Fritz Goldberg is a skinny, naked man, who needs to learn respect for other humans, especially his spouse and child.

We've now been 'round the world in classic fashion: This skinny naked man is half **German** and half **Chinese**, bearing a

---

[1] *"Squaw"*, which is not a politically correct word.

very **Jewish** name but imitating radical **Islamic** beliefs, with an **English** named wife and a **Spanish** named son and written about in **American Indian** legends, reported to you by this **Scottish** writer. We truly live in a "Melting pot of the **World**".

If anyone out there thinks they would like to give "house-sitting" a try, we can give you a great recommendation!

Al Allaway

Chapter Thirteen: *"Okra for Labor Day"*

(Abraham Lincoln: "I have been driven many times to my knees by the overwhelming conviction that I had absolutely no other place to go.")

Labor Day weekend plans were being made for a big Hawaiian "Luau".

Fritz's masonry engineer was a New Zealander named Sulie and he volunteered to roast the pig, whole! Sulie was the only original construction fellow who was still on the payroll. But I think it was because he and Fritz had been friends for many years, and they knew how to communicate with each other. And Sulie refused to take any crap from Fritz.

Preparations were started for the Luau the week before.

"You pull all the weeds, and clean up the garden, Al," Fritz commanded, "Cut grass extra short and scoop up all dog do."

"And Del," he continued, "Please to prune and dead-head roses and pick off all dead geranium."

"Yes, sir," I said. And thought to myself, that this was the first time I'd ever heard the word **please** out of Fritz in the four and a half months we'd been there. Del and I talked about it later, and she agreed.

Chinese herbs used in cooking, closely resemble some Northwest noxious weeds, and when I got into the wild Goosefoot **(Chenopodium)**, wild Catnip **(Nepeta)** and his prize Horseradish, the icky stuff hit the fan, and Fritz was off on another angry tantrum.

Other jobs that week also had to be moved ahead of schedule, so everything would be ready for a house full of Labor Day guests. He said there were going to be over 50 people, some staying over night. Fritz was no help when he got drunk again.

"I've just vacuumed the bottom of the pool," I told him, "And Juan is down there again digging up the potted palms, and rinsing his spoon in the pool."

Fritz never once laid a hand on the kid, or his dogs, but the rest of us sure took plenty of abuse.

A couple of days before the big party, Millie and Fritz went to some nearby farm to buy produce. They brought home several hundred pounds of corn, squash, melons and other stuff, which sat around in boxes and bags, the refrigerators already being too full with meats (and beer).

They also had a sweet tooth for fresh Roma tomatos, and every time we went shopping, we were supposed to bring back ten pounds or so. But we quit the practice after the third time they "forgot" to reimburse us for their tomatos.

Flies were a terrible problem, the kitchen population usually running somewhere around 300.

I could swat up to five house flies with one blow and I thought of Fritz's future plans to make a Bed & Breakfast. Why, the Health Dept. would have him shut down the first day!

Millie asked Del why there were always so many flies. How can you answer something so obvious? It makes one wonder if there are no flies in China. The simple solution, Del told her, is to chain up the dogs, or put latches on the doors that they couldn't keep opening, and for big and little people to close the doors after them, which would obviously keep most of the flies outside.

To make matters worse, then the wind picked up and the recently cleaned courtyard and garden became littered with trash blown in from the garbage trenches.

The first guests to arrive, were two of Fritz's computer gurus from Seattle; more beer drinking buddies. Both men were assigned the room next to ours, which only had a small double bed. These guys were overly friendly with each other, leaving much open for speculation.

While preparations continued, I was glad that I had job responsibilites to take me out and away from the hub of activities.

Water drip lines covered the upper trees on five of the 300 acres of Fritz's property, and they needed constant attention. Lines would often break, and while waiting for Fritz to repair them, I found myself hauling many buckets of water up the hill to his precious fruit trees. But, I was grateful for the chance to get away from the house.

The "big party day" finally arrived. Fritz had invited all his neighbors, employees and numerous friends. It was a nice day, great for an outdoor Luau, but a day with a message…Nobody showed up! Poor Millie felt the humiliation more that anyone.

Besides the family and the two computer nerds, there was Sulie, who roasted the pig, his wife and Del and I; a total of nine! If we counted the pets, we might have been able to stretch it to sixteen. Rosy was busy with her own family, Victor had been given his walking papers two weeks earlier and Yoo had gone back home to Korea.

It was truly a feast to remember. They fed us Oriental and Polynesian dishes never found in restaurants. Fritz loved to deep-fat fry, and made a specialty of a spicy beer batter with which he coated everything. I would never have believed how tasty okra and brussel sprouts could be, cooked this way. Labor day ended quietly, with beer belches and snores. I don't think Fritz even realized that none of his invited guests ever showed up.

We found it difficult to recall the real purpose of house-sitting; which would be defined as; taking care of property when the owner's are away. In almost five months time there might have been two weeks when we were alone and totally responsible for this millionaire's mansion. Fritz, fortunately for us, was absent more time, maybe two months out of the five.

Feeling that time was running out for the "other shoe to fall", Del and I started reviewing our options. We would have been out of there long ago if it wasn't free rent.

Unknown to them, we were running an ad, hoping to find other accommodations.

And we did, *allelulia!*

It was a vacant, but near new mobile home in Yakima's best, Sun Country Estates. We had tried to buy in there seven years before, to no avail.

In early October, we told Fritz that we planned to buy our own place.

"Can you still sit for me this winter?" he pleaded.

Afraid to open my mouth, fearful of what I might say, I merely shook my head, "**NO!**"

"We'll be leaving for Yuma, Arizona on October 10th," Del told him, "To sell our furniture, and put our home there on the market."

We explained that we would clear all our stuff out of the bedroom before we left, and store it all in another unused room.

"Is that okay?" I asked.

"Ja!"

On October 9th, the day before our planned departure, an early knock woke us. It was Rosy.

"Get up and get dressed," she said, The drapery company is here to measure the windows."

Unbelievable! After we've cooked in here for almost five months!

That afternoon, Fritz announced, "Right now, ve going to Seattle for two days, see you ven ve get back."

I'm still wondering, years later, if I shouldn't have reminded him that we'd be gone before he got back. Because, when we did return at the end of the month, to pick up our stuff and the other car, he wouldn't even speak to us. Two trips, later, we were gone.

In closing, I wish to relate a favorite quote from Mark Twain, who said it like this: *"Persons attempting to find a motive in this narrative will be prosecuted; persons attempting to find a moral in it will be banished; persons attempting to find a plot in it will be shot."*

Snowbirds Guarding the Gold
RV Life & House-Sitting Adventures

The "Dungeon"

(Psalm 71:18 *"Now also when I am old and greyheaded, O God, forsake me not; until I have shewed thy strength unto this generation, and thy power to every one that is to come"*)

The End

About the Author

A native of Portland, Al served in the Navy as a photographer during Korea. He served as staff photographer at University of Portland. Al was then a firefighter, working 911 dispatch and Staff officer.

Al had been collecting nature and scenic photo slides all his life. He and wife, Del traveled in a motor home for ten years after retirement. Travels included all of the Western states working membership campgrounds and resorts. Al wrote eleven programs to go with his slides that were booked into many parks. They met many gospel musicians and entertainers. It was their summertime house-sitting adventures and the odd people they met, which stimulated the writing of this book.

Printed in the United States
883800004B